Debbie,
Thank you
for comi-
today!

MW00717404

PICKING UP THE

PIECES

H*of*OPE

MARIANNE STONE

PICKING UP THE PIECES *of* HOPE

TATE PUBLISHING
AND ENTERPRISES, LLC

Published by Tate Publishing & Enterprises, LLC
127 E. Trade Center Terrace | Mustang, Oklahoma 73064 USA
1.888.361.9473 | www.tatepublishing.com

Tate Publishing is committed to excellence in the publishing industry. The company reflects the philosophy established by the founders, based on Psalm 68:11,
"The Lord gave the word and great was the company of those who published it."

Book design copyright © 2014 by Tate Publishing, LLC. All rights reserved.
Cover design by Rtor Maghuyop
Interior design by Joana Quilantang

Published in the United States of America

ISBN: 978-1-62854-104-5
1) Body, Mind & Spirit / Spirituality / General
2) Biography & Autobiography / Personal Memoirs
14.05.20

Please notice the differentiation between Joey and his father, Joe. However, some names have been changed throughout this book. Certain circumstances have been purposely omitted to respect other people's privacy. All of the facts are an accurate account of the developments that occurred.

DEDICATION

I dedicate this book to my family.
Our road has been long with peaks as well as very deep valleys.
Our lessons have been hard. Our strength has been tested.
As we continue to weather the storm, love within creates unity.
We pick up the pieces one at a time and remember.
Thank you.

Hope is something you cannot see
Resting dormant deep within you
It seems misplaced when you need it most
But it is there
Be ready for the moment it awakes
Seize it ever so tightly
So it does not slip from within your grasp
Embrace it courageously
Igniting your beacon of guiding strength
For hope has the ability to carry you to places
You never thought possible
Remember, it is something
You already possess
Never to be surrendered
Reawaken it, cherish it
Know it is *real*.

THE WIND BENEATH
OUR WINGS

A love that is so strong
Carries you through lessons
You reluctantly must learn
Its power shows you, you can go on
It engulfs and strengthens you
To your surprise, you discover
Much of the strength you claim is your own!

CONTENTS

FOREWORD

How do I describe an inspiration, a true heroine who has embraced an intangible love that only heaven can bring? That love, which cannot be seen or heard, continues to consume our hearts and minds. This is a make-or-break kind of love especially when a mother loses a child. The heroine is Marianne Stone. The inspiration is her story of experiencing the passing of her only son and firstborn child, Joey.

I am a spiritual medium, which means I am the voice of those whom have crossed over from this world and reside in heaven. I am able to communicate with them and relay messages to loved ones on earth.

I first met Marianne eleven years ago when I was reading for a group of her family and friends. It was hosted by her cousin Julie. We were all strangers when we met but ended the night as friends. I noticed her right away, for she smiled at me as I came through the door. She was (and still is) a physically beautiful, bright-eyed woman with a warm smile. She seemed very relaxed and open.

Marianne was the first to receive a few messages from a kindly grandmother with words of love and encouragement. Moving on, I continued to deliver messages to every person in the room with ease and abundance. Curiously, I kept getting drawn back to Marianne, but once with her, I was almost tongue tied as if I wasn't meant to speak to her or what was trying to come through was not meant to be spoken. I could feel Marianne's frustration and hope as well, for I was sure she had a lot of questions. It wasn't until the group session ended some three hours later that I immediately approached

Marianne and told her sometimes this happens and that there must be a reason for it. She was gracious and understanding, and she proceeded to ask me spiritual questions. We had a nice conversation. The night ended, and we parted ways. A pleasant memory of Marianne remained branded in my mind, and I never forgot her face.

Six months later, I received a frantic phone call from her cousin Julie, who was sobbing hysterically. Marianne's only son, Joey, had tragically drowned, and the worst devastation followed. That was in April of 2002. Eleven years have come and gone so quickly. It was hard to imagine that from that first meeting at the group session in October 2001, I would be witness to a true miracle! Shortly after the tragedy, I was privileged to do readings for Marianne and her husband, Joseph, although this time, it was in the hopes of channeling divine messages from Joey.

It was a humbling experience for me, and I valued their trust through the worst pain of their lives. I prayed for Joey to come through. He never disappointed! Powerful, precise, and filled with love, Joey reached out from heaven to not only heal his mother's shattered heart but his whole family, friends, teachers, and all those who even knew of him as well. If there was ever a hero to a heroine, it is Joey Stone! For, you see, that is what Joey Stone was all about. In life, he was called Superman! He was a football hero, a friend to all, a champion for the underdog, a protector of those who were bullied or demeaned. He was a loyal friend, funny, as well as generous and caring. Not to mention, he was very handsome too! He was a son who was also a best friend to his mom, dad, and four sisters. Is it any wonder he would be as big in spirit as he was in life? No wonder at all. For through the power of love, Joey was able to break through any barriers between heaven and earth and reach across time to deliver a wonderful gift to his mother. He passed his torch onto her. He instilled in her the great belief that no life is wasted and that his was meant to touch as many lives as possible in powerful, meaningful ways during his short eighteen years. And through signs and continued messages, he would help guide her into fulfilling her destiny, which is to be an inspiration and healer to all those who suffer in this school of life, to help others who have lost their child in sudden tragedies, to be selfless, not selfish, and to rise above her own pain and utilize it as a tool of empathy to ease the suffering of others.

I didn't know Joey Stone in life, but I know him now in ways that are humbling, and I bear witness to a son's ultimate love and devotion to his mother. Marianne has taken her son by the hand and walks with him in truth and harmony. She acknowledges his special signs—his football jersey number 34! She, without guile or ego, has stepped out of her own comfort zone and studied and gathered spiritual knowledge and teachings, something she would have never done if Joey had not "gone home" so suddenly and opened that door of destiny to her. He has lifted her and empowered her every day along the way over the past eleven years, making her know she is never without his guidance and love by communicating not only with me but with his four beautiful sisters through dreams and many wonderful visitations.

He rewards his mother with proof of life everlasting and the importance to celebrate each and every life to remember him not as he left but as he lived and to arm her with the power of love and forgiveness. And because all life matters, because all life has a purpose, she must honor his and hers by being committed to the truth of each soul's purpose, and that truth is to help mankind, to be that champion, that hero or heroine to all who suffer in every way. Marianne knows this truth to be self-evident. She has devoted her time and energy to helping each and every person, friends and strangers alike, not only with the gifts that Joey has instilled in her but also with acute kindness. After meeting Marianne, everyone walks away a better person. You instantly feel it, know it, and believe!

Make no mistake, Marianne suffered deeply, for Joey was the very breath in her body and his passing could have taken her with him. It could have made her life a depressive, dysfunctional void. But she made a choice. She chose to believe. She chose to receive. She chose to acknowledge the truth of her son's incredible existence even through time and space and share the love and joy that not only surrounds Joey in heaven but the love and joy that he is. What better purpose on earth than to care for our fellow man and to share all the gifts God has bestowed upon us. Marianne, recognizing that, turned the greatest tragedy of her life into the most inspirational example of love and human kindness that I have ever witnessed or ever will. This is the miracle! This is the true and accurate story of a son's love for his mother so great that it will change your lives in wondrous ways too and it will open your mind and senses to all the realities of life after death and how each and everyone can be compelled to reach deep inside and find their own special gifts too, gifts of kindness and love.

The world is weary, and many tragedies from Mother Earth and also human hands are likely to happen. We will all be called to expand our minds and open our hearts and become our own heroes and heroines, and there is no doubt after reading this book that you will also come to believe. Marianne Stone is the inspiration and has opened that same door to each and every one of you that her loving son Joey opened up to her. I'm proud to have been a part of Marianne's journey and metamorphosis these past eleven years. I can't wait to see what the next eleven years will bring. I'm blessed to know her and even more blessed to call her my bestest. She has humbled me as I watched and continue to watch her. She is a true healer! A true heroine. Enjoy, embrace, and God bless you all in love and light.

—Marti

INTRODUCTION

This is a story of hope found as a mother and her family are faced with hopelessness. This is about discovering accumulated strength along a path through faith and validation and proving that love conquers all and is always offered from our loved ones in spirit.

Your steps toward healing depend on you. When we are willing to open an accepting heart, it is then when we are strengthened with the healing love of hope. Follow me in my discovery while embracing a continual unwavering bond of love from heaven.

The enclosed occurrences may be difficult for some people to accept. Many may simply slam this book closed and just sum it up to nonsense. My intention is not to alter anyone's individual beliefs. I am just delivering the developments as they unfolded with 100 percent accuracy. My advice would be to take what feels right with you and leave the rest behind.

CHAPTER 1

A MOTHER'S PROTECTION

Children are priceless jewels we love
and cherish through life
Parading them proudly so all can view
Each jewel has many facets enhancing
its natural born beauty
As you care and polish with a nurturing tenderness
An essence peaks through
Even more brilliantly beautiful
Than you could have ever possibly imagined

I can still clearly remember the first day I held my precious son within my locked arms on July 13, 1983. He was brought to me wrapped tightly in his newborn blanket with only his tiny head visible. The thick strawberry-blonde hair upon his head and the small wrinkled face instantly melted my heart. I quickly knew our lives had become richly enhanced. We named our son after his father and mine, Joseph Nicholas Stone. Soon, we all called him Joey. As I focused upon his innocence, deep within my consciousness blossomed a vow of protecting him from all harm. What love and awe my husband and I felt for this little stranger. Realizing now, we were the proud parents of a firstborn son into our newly formed family. Before this day, we both had dreamed of a full family. It was especially my wish for a son to be born first. Not that we wouldn't have been overjoyed if our first born was a girl, but I had lived that role long ago. As I reflected upon my own young life, being the oldest of five, I had very large shoes to fill. I am among three other sisters and one brother. With guidance and protection remaining important to me, I quickly became a tomboy. Being a girl didn't help me, so as a result I found myself in many circumstances defending my siblings. I pulled it off very well, but the thought of handing it over to an older brother of strength would have made it a little easier. Now the wish for my own family had come true!

I can still recall some of Joey's interests when he grew a little older. The *He-Man* was a big hit around the time he was in early elementary school. He was a huge super hero. The impressions Joey often enacted (as best he could) always made my husband and I laugh. Every afternoon when his father was at work, Joey and I were sure to tune in. Not too soon after, we moved into the *Ninja Turtles* craze, then it was *GI Joe*. Saving the world seemed to always appeal to Joey. Afternoons he would jump off the school bus, leap into my arms, and then run to the door, hoping not to miss a minute of each episode.

As the years went on, we also became parents to four beautiful girls, whom we also love very much. Our eldest daughter, Isabelle, was born a few years after Joey. Fifteen months later followed Lynn. They both were blondes along with beautiful big blue eyes.

These two sisters had a lot of fun with their brother as he did with them. I remember the typical teasing as all siblings do. I especially recall a night just prior to their bedtime. I had heard a commotion between the three of them coming from the other side of the house. I approached them and heard Isabelle whining, "Joey said I'm not a cool cat!" Of course he was referring to how she was regarded among her peers at school. (You know, being cool was very important while growing up.) At first, I heard the chuckle under his breath as he was enjoying her dismay. Without much further hesitation though, he assured her it wasn't true, apologized, and offered her words of confidence and reassurance. He didn't take enjoyment in seeing his sisters upset. To this day, I often laugh and remind her of that experience. These are perfect examples of the bonds between siblings and the love and joy they shared among them.

The dedication of protection he had for his sisters started early in Joey's life. I remember when Joey had attended a day camp at the nearby school during the summer months. All their peers attended, and there was no cost at the time, so it became a huge meeting place. This day, Isabelle and Lynn both joined him. He was on the other side of a field with his friends when Lynn got into a little scuffle with a boy! Now, Lynn was a tomboy very much like myself. However, this older boy, who started a fight, was going to find out before long whose sister she was, and he was clearly biting off more than he could chew! He threw some water at her as he proceeded tormenting her through nonstop teasing. Somehow, one of Joey's friends got wind of the commotion and told him. He was quickly running over to defend his little sister. As he approached the scene, he was shocked to see Lynn had turned an empty rubber garbage container on top of this boy, who quickly became very upset! As the can was removed, it was clear he was fine but a little humiliated. Joey and his friends found it funny that even though Lynn was little, she was able to defend herself. Stone was a fitting name now, even for a girl.

Some four years later, I received the shock of my life when I learned I was expecting twins! My husband and I were thrilled while at the same time a little nervous of how our family size would expand so quickly to five children. As our excitement and anticipation grew toward their arrival, so did Joey's. He secretly was hoping to get a brother out of the deal. Through the technology of ultrasound, it wasn't too long after that I discovered he would soon have four sisters. Joey wasn't upset; I know at the time he imagined he would feel outnumbered, but that quickly changed. He loved his other sisters and very much liked being referred as the big brother, so what did two more matter?

When the twin girls were born by an emergency cesarean section, there were some serious complications affecting one of them, Gabrielle. Evidently, there was some oxygen deprivation. Our whole family was on standby with an overwhelming continual worry. Hours after her birth, she was quickly transferred to another hospital that was better equipped to meet her needs. Gianna, her twin sister, was also in slight distress following her birth, but it was a less serious circumstance. Each family member took a shift at our house helping out with the three other children while also visiting Gianna and me, who were still at the hospital. They also visited Gabrielle who remained in newborn intensive care.

Gianna was the first baby to leave the hospital when I was released. As my husband and I arrived home, we walked through the door for the first time with our latest addition. Gianna was quickly transferred to the welcoming arms of her sisters and brother.

Yet we all still spent a lot of time at the hospital caring and feeding Gabrielle while at the same time attending to Gianna's needs at home. It was touch and go for a while. Thankfully Gabrielle pulled through, and a week later, she was also on her way home with us. As we walked in the door once again now with Gabrielle, Joey was patiently waiting again with his arms open to finally hold another sister. We all knew how lucky we were since she had been so very close to death. The doctors offered us plenty of encouragement for Gabrielle's full recovery. We all believed there would be no further complications as a result of her difficulties so early in her life. The thought of a brother was certainly long forgotten, as Joey quickly became my right-hand man at the tender age of nine while my husband was at work. I certainly didn't put any demands on him, but he was always by my side and offering his help. I often enjoyed seeing him hugging and kissing the babies unconditionally, even changing them. He always showed them tender loving care.

Our family unit was a very happy and secure home. The circle of love was now complete. Joey's younger sisters throughout life would always feel very loved and protected by their older brother. His heart always remained in the right place, never wavering.

Approximately four years later, it became abundantly clear that Gabrielle was in need of a corrective surgery to one of her legs. She had worn braces for a few years and received physical and occupational therapy three times a week, at Easter Seals.

The doctor diagnosed her with mild Cerebral Palsy. He explained this sometimes occurs after a traumatic birth, such as Gabrielle's.

Gabrielle's condition was affecting her walking ability, which made her movement difficult. The surgery she needed would correct this and remove the need for the leg braces.

So again she was off for a hospital stay. Gabrielle and I spent almost a week there. It was very painful at times for her. Once home, we soon realized it would be quite sometime for her to recover. Joey carried her everywhere as her leg began to heal. Her three sisters entertained her and pushed her around in a wheelchair within our home. When the girls were doing homework or were not at home for some reason, Joey would place Gabrielle on the couch next to him. They would enjoy a show, or he would just spend time talking to her. Joey truly filled the role as a great brother.

With all of Joey's loving ways, he still though was very much a typical boy. There is an experience that proves this and one I will never forget. As he attended school, Joey always would work hard to maintain his good grades. I can remember one year while in the middle school that he had an especially hard time in science class. When he returned home from school one day, he entered the house holding his report card. He handed it to me; I anxiously began to absorb the anticipated results. As I quickly scrolled down the page, I noticed he had an A, a few B's and two Cs. Science, which had been such a struggle at the time, had received a B!

My husband and I were pleased. I again scrolled down the page with glee. Then something odd caught my eye, so I strained to look a little closer. I couldn't believe my eyes! It appeared that one of the Bs didn't look quite right. Joey quickly admitted he changed the D into a B! We both looked at him in disbelief. We weren't angry, just a little shocked at the lengths he took to change the situation. Then I reminded myself of how children really want to please their parents. So we spoke to him with care and explained how we knew this subject was a struggle for him, and it was okay. The next semester, we would study together a little more, and with his best effort, we knew he would do fine. He agreed and assured us he wouldn't repeat that stunt again. We knew when the next report card arrived it would prove to be true. My husband and I still chuckle as we recall this experience. I have to admit, my husband, Joe, used his own means to help give Joey a boost. I was quickly informed by them both of how his dad had made a secret deal with him. Joey was expected to improve and complete the year with all passing grades. As a result, his dad would buy him a special gift. Although not too long after, I realized the gift they agreed on was also for the both of them. He knew Joey loved sports as did he, so he offered Joey a baseball pitching machine and cage of his own! You guessed it: all the future report cards were a majority of Bs and a couple of As. That next baseball season, it was in our backyard. It had proved to add a great incentive to our deal.

Joey seemed to do especially well playing baseball with all the practice he received. His love for baseball continued to intensify. Soon, Joey became a hard hitter and very much enjoyed being a part of the baseball team. His nickname quickly became Clobber, while in the middle school. Not too long after that, many of his neighborhood friends were in our yard, all enjoying the benefits of the pitching machine.

Sports in general were important to Joey. He had an ability much like his dad, doing well at all he participated in. So the variety broadened greatly as did his ability to become an asset to the teams he joined. As a family unit, we had attended many basketball, baseball, and football games. We all cheered as we watched our Joey play. If he wasn't playing the sport, he was watching one on television or attending a game with his dad. Joey and his father were dedicated Boston Red Sox fans. The trips they made together to attend these games were always a blast. As far as football went, he joined his father's loyalty and dedication for the Saint Louis Rams. Through a friend's help, my husband was not only able to bring Joey to a Rams game but he also was able to meet a few of the players. He was in awe as he finally met the players he had collected all the stats on at home within his many sports cards. This was very much appreciated by Joey; they had a wonderful time. They always had a close-knit father-and-son bond.

As Joey entered into the high school, he connected well to many of his peers. I can still recall his friends phoning him, requesting advice for their own relationship problems. Somehow, he always knew what support and direction to offer them. He paced while on the phone as he wholeheartedly listened carefully. He became matchmaker, and still today many relationships continue. Within his own life, he had only short-term relationships. It wasn't that he was unable to; it was more because he didn't wish to. It was like an inner knowing; that this just wasn't in the cards for him. It seemed as if he had a much greater scope to accomplish while maintaining friendships with others.

As my husband and I attended a parent night visit to his teachers, I stood in amazement of the admiration he extended to them. As he introduced us, we felt the loving admiration for us in return. The sincere care and respect he gave was always genuine. We were so proud, and I remembered I wasn't like that in high school, and neither was his father. I'm not saying we were disrespectful, but our intention just wasn't that focused as Joey's was. It just seemed he had many more attributes than I can list. We certainly offered him direction, but to put it honestly, my husband and I cannot fully take credit for all he had already become at such a young age.

Sports still remained very important to Joey. He supported his classmates by attending as many games as he could. The girls, or the guys—it didn't matter—you could always count on Joey cheering from the stands. Football, however, had somehow become a major focus and the only sport I was always a little apprehensive about. His desire to play had begun while he was in the middle school. Now though in high school, I guess what troubled me most was the boys were bigger and hit harder. I didn't want my son hurt, but this sport soon became his passion, and Joey was certainly up for this enjoyed challenge as his body and strength grew. It was as if he was driven by some directing force. As he competed, he always did very well, there seemed to be no stopping him. He achieved many awards as well as status throughout the years. Upon the football season of 2001, he had also become an all-state middle linebacker. This senior season was the year of team-accumulated efforts, resulting in great accomplishments! I believe now that there was much going on behind the scenes, with things we couldn't possibly realize then, a dose of heavenly help. Because this year, memories were created and lessons were being taught without even knowing it! I reflect back and now find it no surprise that their football uniforms and school color was amethyst. (This is a very high spiritual color, which represents protection.)

They completed a 10–0 season that year. Each teammate had come from within our small town, uniting with their own unique talents. They each played with such heart and determination. It is hard to explain, but when our boys came on the field, suddenly it was as if you were a family. You felt a surge of euphoria that ran through the players as well as the parents and fans! Prior to each game, the team stood at full attention while the National Anthem was playing. Upon the conclusion, Joey always unleashed his own created Tarzan roar. It's funny how it instilled a wave of confidence among his teammates. A contagious courage spread and kept them united. Throughout the game, no matter how hard an opponent was tackled, there was always a hand extended to pull him to his feet again by him or a teammate. That would usually be followed by a pat on the back. Together they went on to win every game even the second round of the playoffs, then losing the last. The final state championship game was lost to a very tough and player-recruited team.

The abilities our boys had along with the heart and soul of each teammate pulled together very much as a brotherhood. My husband and I were proud to be parents among the others. When I reflect on it now, it has some similarities to what I now refer to as the game of life. At times, you may feel like you are incapable of meeting a challenge; however, when you support one another, miracles happen!

I can recall at a home game how Joey thought of me as he spoke to a friend on the sideline just prior to kick off. He motioned to me with a wave of his hand, although I wasn't sure what his reference was at the time. Then his friend took the coat Joey was wearing as he handed it over to him, and he quickly ran it up to me. I realized Joey knew I was probably cold and he was thinking of his mom. I was so grateful as I put my arms through the sleeves while feeling the love my son has for me while the warmth of his body had still remained within this coat. Boy, I thought for a moment how the tables had turned as he grew older and was now becoming a man. I proudly wore his jacket while trying to contain my beaming ear-to-ear smile.

I continued watching Joey closely; keeping his safety was always a top priority. I even held off allowing him to receive his driver's license until the age of eighteen. This was a big step and I wanted to be sure he was ready and would always be cautious of other experienced drivers. Even this, I know sometimes is not enough. In life, there are no guarantees. I now ponder on some of our conversations Joey would kiddingly say to me.

"Mom, you'll probably come and cut up my dinner meat for me when I'm on my honeymoon."

It still brings a smile to my face when I remember this, but I certainly understood his point. I was truly obsessed; my family is *very* precious to me. While attending all of Joey's football games, my husband would secretly be making deals with God, pleading to always ensure our son's safety. Each and every one of his junior- and senior-year games were videotaped by him. Joe always admired his son's dedication, which poured into each and every game. We were all so proud of our Joey. It seemed everything was really coming together while he still maintained at an above average academic level in school. I had helped promote his college exposure by sending copies of all his best performance games along with his high school transcripts to the coaches on his college prospect list. He had aspirations of studies falling somewhere within the human anatomy field, such as a Physical Therapist or a Chiropractor to help people with sports related injuries.

Joey's position in his senior year for the football team was on both sides of the game. He filled the cleats of a fullback player on the offense and middle linebacker on the defensive side of the competition. My heart soared with pride at each game our family attended. It seemed I remained all consumed, with anticipation for his promising future on many levels. It remained on my mind 100 percent of the time. While college was a priority for Joey, he really didn't want to be too far a distance from his family and friends. Decision time was quickly closing in. He had many choices.

Joey had been accepted to all of the colleges he had applied to. The many packages offered to him were all tempting. There would be little cost to attend. It seemed as if the phone was ringing off the hook in our home with college coaches calling. Opportunity continued knocking, loudly! They had spoken to him at great lengths of time trying to convince him their school was the best choice for him. Graduation was only two months away. He would be nineteen years old in July. All our dreams and hopes were soon to become a reality. All that would change one day, no matter how much I protected him.

April 18, the day after my birthday, would be etched in my mind forever. Instead of my family planning a celebration, we would be attending a parent's worst nightmare!

CHAPTER 2

OUR SHOOTING STAR

A soul that shines so bright needs no instruction
Lessons learned long ago,
longing only to awaken our hearts
To acknowledge what is important
and cherish it within us
The instructions become evident
As many of our greatest teachers walk among us
Then in an instant are no longer visible
Through this pain the lessons begin.

As I further introduce my son and the love he shared with many, I want to reinforce the fact that he was by no means a mamsey pamsey. He was a very complex young man. Sometimes when a man exhibits compassion, it somehow becomes confused with weakness. This was far from the truth for him. There was always a genuine tenderness and devotion of strength filled loyalty displayed, throughout his many selfless actions. This was especially true for his family and friends, who had grown to count on a forever bond of friendship as well as love from him. If you had newly met him, you would instantly sense a spark of acceptance. Joey had a magnetic way of melting the walls of separation as he initiated new friendships.

It has been said by many people how love sent through laughter can become contagious. Many times you are sharing it without actually being aware of the bonds being mended concurrently. Joey will always be remembered with his explosive sense of humor blending with the force of strength within him. Still he always remained modest while exhibiting his God-given attributes. He was never one to come home and boast of the endeavors of his day. Joey remained a leader and a humble man, not choosing his actions as if filling some egotistical agenda. He just loved others.

I believe the essence of our personality, which makes us who we are, is carried with us even in death. This example will give you a glimpse of the bonds he shared with many. Joey's vibrant personality explodes, and I become again filled in this laughter as I sometimes replay a video of him. This isn't all that often because it also comes with a price. It pulls at my heart reminding me of my treasured son and wishing, I could somehow go back in time.

In high school, every year, Joey's Italian class would perform a skit. Everyone in the class performed a specific role. Each would forge together a collection of music and have it played as they entered the room. Then of course they had to speak with the Italian dialogue. Joey had built a great rapport with his teachers. For this Italian teacher, it was especially true as he had attended her progressing class for a number of years. This senior year of Joey's though, was very different. He would play the role of impersonating the teacher, and that meant dressing as a woman. As the skit began, he came into the classroom wearing an oversized black tunic dress of mine. To carry his ensemble, he had his Aunt Toni's pearl earrings clasped on his ears and shoes (which clearly didn't fit) on his feet. He also wore his great-grandmother's pearl necklace, which gave him the finishing touch for just the right look. He poured much thought into every area to pull it off spectacularly. He wanted to precisely mimic his teacher's daily routine, but of course exaggerate his display. Or it wouldn't be funny.

The music he chose was the whistle hymn from the opening to the *Andy Griffith Show* of many years ago. As he entered the classroom, he shimmied over to the teacher's desk and began his part as the teacher. He shouted out instructions to the students in the Italian language. Their role was to give him a hard time. The excitement of watching Joey trying to contain his classmate's hilarity was captivating. Soon a wrestling match erupted; truly they were all enjoying it. After a very short time, Joey was trying to separate them and control his laughter. Before all was said and done, the classroom broke into complete hysteria.

The electricity of that video truly exhibits the magnetism of Joey. This short skit captured the down-to-earth young man he was. It was how he had connected to people and enjoying the friendships created that really mattered most to him. He wasn't concerned with one's status, or how well he knew you. If you needed him, he was there. Social boundaries were nonexistent to Joey.

While Joey's humor was quite common in the classroom, appropriate timing had to also call for it. If a lesson was complete, he took advantage of it often. He was well liked by all the teachers as he was always respectful in return.

Joey was a huge WWF fan. Many nights he remained glued to the television along with his sister Gabrielle, as usual by his side, enjoying every minute of the show. Trying wrestling moves on each other was always funny since he was nine years older than her. Yet Joey always remained gentle.

On another particular day in high school, as the class was ending, Joey flooded the room exhibiting his spontaneous sense of humor. While there was a moment of quiet opportunity, he quickly stood up with his arms drawn and his fists clenched. He began demonstrating his best impression of the The Rock (who was a WWF participant at the time) while flexing his muscles simultaneously. Then he yelled, "Can you smell what The Rock is cooking?" Everyone broke out into laughter. With his name being Joey Stone and often just referred to as Stone, this probably added to the humor of him mimicking The Rock.

Joey's devotion to connections while in school also extended beyond his classmates. If he had noticed any of his family visiting his high school, he immediately welcomed them with warmth. This also always included his sisters. He was never embarrassed by their presence while in another's company. He always remained very proud of them.

Once, I recall stopping at the high school to visit my aunt. She worked in the cafeteria. She was known to all as; Joey's Auntie Toni. Many of his friends addressed her in the same manner. I was speaking to her on that particular day. I had my young twin daughters with me; they were about six years old. Earlier, we all had attended a meeting within the school. When the lunch bell rang, it wasn't long before I heard Joey's voice roaring down the hallway approaching us. He was surrounded by his friends. I thought to myself, *I won't bother him.* Then he quickly walked over and leaned down. He then scooped up each child, one in each arm, and off to the cafeteria they went. He proudly carried them to greet the rest of his friends. I could hear his laughter as he shared the joy he found, joking with his sisters while in the company of his friends.

The close connection of love he had with his Auntie Toni often spread to others through they're similar sense of humor. One afternoon at the end of the day, she was running late as Joey passed by the cafeteria on his way out. Now she was aware of Joey not having a driver's license as of yet, but he was attending driver's education classes. Auntie Toni then asked him to start her car. After a few minutes she and another employee proceeded to enter the school parking lot. Something odd caught her attention as then she tried to focus her eyes on an outrageous site! Her friend burst out laughing as she saw her car drive by! Apparently Joey didn't stop with just starting the car. He now was driving the car with four other friends in it! As he passed where Auntie Toni was standing, she only saw arms and legs, but she heard her name as they all shouted, "Hi, Auntie Toni!"

Well, Joey must have seen the shocked expression on her face, so he pulled over to pick her up! Now since everyone was safe, she was trying to contain her laughter. She could never really get mad at Joey; because she loved him deeply. So she motioned for him to move in, and she assumed the driver's seat. It was a joke among her coworkers; however, she never asked him to start her car at school again!

While Joey's sense of humor was a way for him to touch many hearts, he also had a very serious side to him. I had heard that one of my distant cousins whose family had lost touch with ours was now a new teacher at Joey's high school. I told him to look for her by her last name among the new teachers even though he hadn't met her yet. Shortly after that, he located her and was sure to introduce himself as a cousin. Soon it was required for him to include the very subject she would be teaching within his required school credits. So he became a student in her classroom and was thrilled for the opportunity. He soon learned she had two children attending school in another town where she had lived. Her daughter was the oldest and closest to Joey's age. One night, he picked up the telephone, called her, and introduced himself, creating a strengthened family reconnection. He then encouraged his cousin to call him if she needed him. Over time, a great family bond had formed between them all.

The following year the family moved into town, and his cousin enrolled within his school. All learned that she was Joey Stone's cousin and welcomed her. This was a clear example of how Joey connected to his family. I soon learned just how important it is to acknowledge all the love and relationships you have in your life right now. Always remember to appreciate what is so precious. The memories of love shared are what you retain.

Much later, I came to realize hardships transform us to become lessons learned toward strengthening the soul.

LOVE

Love is something everyone is sharing
Love is better than anything
Love is something that keeps us alive
Love is joy and happiness
Love is always being shared
Love is life
Some people think money is better than love, but they're wrong
You don't need money to be happy, *you need love*
When people die, they can still feel your love
Even though you can't see them, you can still feel their love
A part of them is always in your heart
Their bodies go, but their souls don't
They can see you, and feel your pain
Love is *very* special
I am loved by many people
Even if you don't know it, you are always being loved
Your mother will always be with you
Robin Strickland
(This was written when she was eight years old.)

CHAPTER 3

THE TRAGEDY

When the unthinkable has the power
To cripple even the mightiest
The cost of love is delivered
Through a searing pain
Once, face-to-face with loss
A scream resonates so loud within you
That you can no longer decipher the words
A part of you taken forever
To *never* completely heal
Decided as an injustice to innocence
April 18, 2002

This day started out like any other. Joey's friend called him and asked him to join a few others. They were going to meet at a pond. There was a huge heat wave going on, so it seemed to be a good idea to him. He had many other prior obligations, which seemed to fall apart that day. He should have been attending a track meet. (He was also the track captain of the team.) The meet was canceled. Then a football practice was suddenly rescheduled for another day. These obligations would have kept him far from the pond. But it was just too hot, it was a freak weather pattern. This almost never occurs—ninety-degree temperatures in April. I remember this day so clearly. It will remain etched in my mind forever. It was the day before was my forty-second birthday. I recall Joey coming home with a card for me in his hands. He stopped where he was, turned to me, and said "Happy Birthday, Mom." I will cherish that card forever.

My son was always an awesome swimmer. He took lessons when he was much younger, and we also owned a pool for quite a few years. His body was in top shape, muscle bound, and with almost zero body fat. He was always in the gym due to football.

That day, Joey and his friends went out for a day expected to be filled with fun. They drove to a popular pond in the next town. The day of fun had somehow turned into a day of horror they will never forget. As to just what exactly went wrong, I may never know every detail; however later, we received an explanation from a doctor. He began by saying that due to Joey having almost-zero body fat and the water temperature being so very cold, it affected his heart and caused his arms and legs not to work properly.

As a result, he was unable to save himself and his friends didn't realize the seriousness, until it was too late. However, I do know his friends would never want harm to come to him. Tragically, our Joey slipped away from us that day. It was like the hand of God took Joey's hand and brought him home to heaven.

I had arrived home from shopping with my daughter and my Auntie Toni. After all, I still was in that birthday mode. All that came to a screeching halt as I drove into my driveway and noticed a police car waiting there. As soon as I parked, my husband came rushing out of the house.

He said, "Joey's been in an accident."

I thought, *Oh no, he's been in a vehicular accident*, never thinking anything worse than a few scrapes since, after all, my son was a Stone and we are all tough. My denial was keeping me sane as the same thought rushed again and again through my mind and my whispers barely touched my lips, "He'll be okay. He'll be okay."

I attempted to remain calm as my husband was breaking the speed limit. As we became closer to the hospital, my worry suddenly began to grow. So then I did what I always relied on doing: I prayed to God. As I felt panic squeaking in, next I spoke to my deceased grandmother under my breath. I kept pleading over and over, "Please keep my Joey safe. Please help him!" Then I prayed all the prayers I could think of over and over.

At the hospital, they wouldn't give us any answers. A nurse came and led us down the hallway. My knees became weak after I looked into her eyes. A wave of my worst fear engulfed me. I then pleaded, "PLEASE JUST TELL ME MY SON IS OKAY!" When she didn't reassure me, I suddenly felt my body becoming numb. She and my husband then began to pull me forward down the hallway toward a room as my legs ceased working properly.

This extreme fear now consumed every inch of me as my heart pounded loudly. After a few minutes, a doctor came into the room. She announced what seemed so easily to roll off her tongue, "He drowned."

A blood-curdling screech leaped out of the deepest part of my being, louder than I could have ever imagined. I then collapsed to the floor face down. All I could do was scream over and over again, "NOT MY JOEY! NOT MY JOEY! HE PROMISED ME! HE PROMISED!"

Family was arriving now, and my husband and I were in pieces! There was little else to say. We were beyond despair! How will we survive? How will I survive? I had always asked Joey to promise me nothing would ever happen to him. I would tell him, I could never survive it and I would join him. And now that day has arrived! He always promised.

Maybe somewhere deep inside my soul somehow I knew. That would explain why I was so overprotective. How could this happen? I kept thinking of my other children. How will I tell them? How will we survive? He meant so much to all of us! "Oh God, how could you let this happen? We don't deserve this!" I kept saying even though now I know that's not how it works. But it kept ringing in my head. My complete despair totally overwhelmed me! It seemed as if I would never stop screaming, especially as I saw the pain in my husband's eyes. The pain in my heart was all too much! I could not contain my hysteria.

The doctors then asked if I wanted to see him. Another extreme rush of panic hit me and a shriek leapt from my body, "Noooo!" This was beyond anything I could even think of for even a second. No way would I ever be able to handle seeing my precious son this way. (However, my husband Joe and my sister Linda, did chose to visit Joey and spend time with his lifeless body.) Suddenly, I recalled how I always thought I had protected him so well. There was nothing but bleakness and confusion to look forward to now.

My husband soon returned and collected his strength enough to remind me that we needed somehow to get home to our other children. He said we needed to tell them before anyone else did. As I am writing this, much time has passed, and I'm still in a fog. Like a part of me that has become numb. It's just too painful. I barely remember the ride home as we both cried uncontrollably, all the way there. As we entered our home once we arrived, we both crept up the stairs to our other children. How painful that conversation was as our daughters rushed to us for some news. (People that had gotten wind of the tragedy had been calling our house previous to our arrival.) Grief and complete despair erupted throughout our home.

Within a very short time, many friends and family were at our door—some people we didn't even know and some friends I remembered from long ago. The news spread like wildfire! Even his high school football coach, who had usually irritated me plenty, was visibly upset upon his visit. He stood in front of me, and all I could do was embrace him and forget my past feelings. They no longer seemed important. There was a constant line of traffic within our home. What love and support we were shown! Yet I have never before still felt so alone! *My God, someone please wake me up! I know I must be having a terrible nightmare! This just can't happen to my Joey! Especially now he had so much opportunity to look forward to. He had worked so hard for his future.*

The high school principal and superintendent soon also visited to pay their respects. They suggested holding a memorial service in the gym for all of Joey's classmates, teachers, and schoolmates. This seemed more appropriate than the traditional wake service.

The impact of loss was so huge to so many people. The announcement press box in the football field was decorated by the students from the high school and friends. There was a huge S painted in red within a Superman diamond. (Many of his friends referred to him also as Superman.) Across the front of the press box read "Home of Joe Stone, class of 2002." His friends also used finger paint to put their palm prints on the press box. Each of them representing their individualized support for Joey yet clinging together as a sense of unity in this time of grief.

Many days later, when I visited, there were many other signs of love for Joey. Many students also left a little individualized message near their palm print. The chain-link fence that ran along the edge of the grass preceding the football field even held a message. Someone spray painted in white. "WE LOVE YOU, JOE" with a huge heart after those words!

I didn't want his friends and family, including us, to increase our suffering if that was at all possible. It was all just so overwhelming, although we welcomed all of the support that was honoring Joey. Uniting us at a school memorial was a good idea so everyone would feel supported. If there was a formal wake service chosen instead, all would have been fixing their eyes upon an empty shell that once contained our precious Joey. I also knew we didn't have the strength to go through that. Just focusing on our love within the high school walls, helped us to lean on each other in attendance.

A day later was the memorial service. As we entered the school, we noticed the walls and hallways had a huge banner of brown paper sprawled across almost all of them. It ran further than the eye could see. Then we noticed many letters written to Joey by students, as they were hanging attached upon the banner, one after the other. The many letters expressed what he meant to them and how he had helped them within their life. Many addressed Joey as their big brother and wrote asking how would they now handle their teenage problems without him. One after another we read them. They all had similarities of how he supported each of them during difficult times within their lives, we were so touched as we pressed ourselves to continue to read them. We quickly noticed this wasn't contained only at Joey's grade level; it had spread throughout the entire school, from the freshman to the senior class. What a legacy of love to be felt by so many!

The gym where the memorial was held in was so overloaded. Teachers from Joey's earlier years were in attendance. Coaches from many years ago were also among the many. Almost every single person came up to us for a hug. They recalled what Joey did for them at one point within their life. There was so much more than we could possibly absorb. It was shocking to see how many people he had inspired. We really weren't aware of the magnitude and the impact felt within this tragedy. It had become bigger than any of us could have anticipated. It clearly represented love.

Two or three of Joey's friends spoke a few words, and then they finished with playing the song "I'll Be Missing You." There wasn't a dry eye in the gymnasium. Our zombie-like bodies were clearly functioning on autopilot. If that wasn't possible, I don't know how we could have gotten through the entire memorial. There is really not much more I can recall from that night. I think I blocked the rest from my memory. The day of the funeral however, would really send us over the edge.

Once we had arrived at the funeral home early on April 21, everyone from the family went inside except for me. I refused to get out of the limousine. I just couldn't bear the thought of seeing my precious son that way. I just flatly refused to accept it. There was no way I could muster the strength, even if I allowed myself to face the pain. So I just sat there. The driver didn't know what to do with me. No coaxing from my husband would work either. I just didn't want to go any further within this escapade. I was battling a tidal wave of pain yet to come. I continued to refuse to accept that my son lay there inside; maybe I thought somehow I could skip over this very painful part. Maybe I thought that the strength of my denial would save me from this nightmare somehow. Then I thought to myself, *I can't and I won't say good-bye!* My refusal remained very firm.

Reluctantly, after a very long while, the driver parked in the back lot and left me there to cry some more. Soon, my mom came to me and finally convinced me to come in and sit where I felt comfortable. (Since there were no calling hours, I figured this would be okay.) I sat in the corner of the room and was frozen with emotion. My children and husband had visited the casket with the pallbearers, who had now arrived. They pleaded with me to walk over, but I couldn't move. I refused. This continued until my husband and sisters said I would regret it for the rest of my life if I didn't. I thought about it for a long while. Then my husband and children led me by the hand, and we approached the casket. I was terrified! This was the first time I would look upon my Joey's lifeless body. Now I did realize I had to, or I wouldn't have been able to convince myself it was real. When I had reached him, he felt so cold. He had become almost unrecognizable. I knew it was not the *real* him. He was no longer inside. I was looking at an empty vessel, which once held the soul of my beloved Joey. It was absolutely horrible! My whole being could not face this. My family was being torn to shreds, and there was nothing I could do about it. It was just way too much to handle.

Our next stop was the funeral mass. Joey's friends were his pall-bearers. The church was so full, standing room only was all that remained. The grief that permeated us all was so enormously thick.

One close friend of Joey's spoke at the church and recalled the bond of friendship they had had. Halfway through his speech, he tried to lighten the heaviness in the room with a tale of Joey as a child and how he always had the best toys. He comically recalled how Joey had all of the figures to the Ninja Turtles and the additional accessories. A sudden wave of laughter for a moment spilled into the church.

Some people were still entering the church a bit late as many were having a very hard time locating a parking space since the lot, as well as the street, was full. Much of it had been blocked off because of the anticipated attendance. I noticed as we were ushered into the limousine once again that the many school buses preparing to leave were also full to capacity. Many students had been bused in from school. The rear window of each bus had a sign. It was colored purple. There was a picture of a football. I read the words: "We will never forget Joe Stone number 34!" I was so touched how they honored my son. As we continued the procession toward the cemetery, we passed the police department and noticed the flag was at the half-mast position. I was overwhelmed with emotion. I recalled the song the organ played during the ceremony, "The Wind Beneath My Wings." I thought to myself that this was a perfect song to describe Joey's actions. As I hear this song today, I always think of my Joey and refer to him as a true hero. This song soon would become one of his many signs.

CHAPTER 4

THE UNBROKEN PROMISE

The sincere trust you place in someone
That can stand the test of time
Never realizing its immeasurable significance
To somehow know you are safe in their care
Sealed within a sacred promise
A vow held through love
Never a second thought of becoming unfulfilled
Cherished for eternity, delivered with trust
And supported in faith
Never to become unbroken
It is the *love* that connects us *all*.

When Joey made a promise to someone, he was sure to keep it. This vow to his mom would be no different. I always remained cautious when it came to my children, however, sometimes they would feel I was overprotective. There was always a final way of finding some peace of mind for me when I would become fearful for their safety. We created a vow of trust and sincere communication between us all. Then we sealed it with two spoken words: "I promise."

This trust we agreed upon was always honored. I was not trying to fool myself; I was a teenager at one time also. So quite often, I was sure to remind him, "Please Joey, be careful. Promise me you won't allow anything to ever take you away from me. I wouldn't survive it."

He would always say, "I promise, Mom."

As soon as those words were spoken, immediately a wave of calm would wash over me. I knew his words were sincere. While in reality I knew there would never be any guarantees, however, he had successfully mastered this skill of calming me. I wanted to forever hold onto my precious son. On the other hand, I could not hold my son so tightly as to not allowing him to be himself. That would not be fair to him. So I always maintained an intuitive bond with him, an even flow of mutual loving compromise. If he stayed out at night late with his friends, I would stop what I was doing and think of him. I would whisper to myself and repeat within my mind, "Joey, call me. Joey, call me. Joey, call me."

Nine times out of ten, he would call me shortly after that or show up at home. I would say to him, "You heard me, didn't you?"

He would chuckle and say, "Yeah, Mom."

Sometimes it was as if he was humoring me, but somehow within us, we both knew and acknowledged the deep connection of love we always shared.

Approximately two weeks before his crossing, I recall a gift I received from him without even realizing it at the time. He was on the computer downstairs, goofing around. I first came into the room and remembered something I needed to do upstairs and proceeded there. As I stepped away from the top step, a wave of unrecognized imminent opportunity came over me. That's the only way I can explain it. I seemed to be compelled to speak to my son. So I immediately turned around and rushed downstairs. As soon as I entered the room I announced how I needed to speak to him. He rolled his eyes as he assumed it was another one of my now-famous household college speeches. Immediately I knew what he was thinking and said, "No, Joey, it's not about college."

"Oh," he quickly replied while exhibiting an obvious smirk and said, "Okay, Mom."

The words I said next just seemed to flow as if they were my last. I don't know any other way to explain it. I felt compelled to pour my heart out to my son. Maybe my anticipation of his soon moving off to college in the near months was a way of dismissing this confusing urge. "I want you to know how proud we are of you. Joey, you are my heart and soul. You are an extension of me. We are so connected. I love you so much."

He said, "I love you too, Mom."

Then the sense of dire need I had prior to this moment instantly became fulfilled. I just smiled and brushed it off. Fully absorbing another wave of love sent from my beloved son and sealed with me inwardly embracing his forever promise of connection. I will remain forever grateful, that I had listened to my intuition that day.

Joey was eighteen years old, three months shy of nineteen, though he acted much older, after all, according to his age; most teenagers are already off to college.

Joey was respectful, intelligent, and always making clear-headed choices. I had no reason to have a strangle hold on him. It was a feeling I needed to learn to live with. Maybe somewhere deep down I might have had an intuitive feeling of actually losing him somehow, so instead I would hold my focus on my own self-reassuring words running through my head over and over, "He'll be okay. He'll be okay." This always helped me, and as a result, I refused to entertain that feeling. I just thought of it as an unfounded fear that most likely resided within the mind of many parents.

On April 18, 2002, as the world came to a screeching halt, those very words "I promise" began to haunt me. I couldn't help myself in the emergency room from screaming, "He promised, he promised!" All that I had always feared was now a reality.

Many hours after family and friends left for home, except for some immediate family members, we turned in for the night. It was surely a waste of time because there would be little sleeping. I knew I was searching for something. I felt as if I had fallen off a huge cliff and needed to grasp something, anything, or I would continue to descend to the darkest of the depths of my forever despair. I needed to somehow know Joey was safe wherever he was and not suffering in any way. I also needed to know that he is still connected to me. I didn't want or could ever give up my being his mom and him as my son, ever! I just simply could not live, if I thought I would never see my beloved son again!

I tried to hold onto the fact that I was always a believer of life after death. As to the many books I had read, there was always mentioning of deceased loved ones visiting in a wonderful dream from the afterlife. I tried to convince myself that this would happen for me and help somehow. Although, I was actually fooling myself into believing I would have a sense of peace no matter how momentary the dream was. The pain was so overwhelmingly more than I could handle, and that was all I could focus on.

I frantically was grasping for any direction reclaiming some kind of connection to my son. So I did the only thing I could do within the confinement of my home: continue to read. I needed to find a momentary peace while my wandering mind could be occupied with some sense of hope. So I began to read everything about the afterlife, looking for hope in real stories from actual people who had also lost loved ones. I was hoping to rekindle my beliefs. I searched for a book I had tucked away from a long time ago that I enjoyed. It was titled *The Séance* by Suzane Northrop. She is a very well-known medium. I had seen her a few times many years ago and watched her in action as she delivered messages from loved ones who've crossed over. It was amazing! She offered real relief to many grieving people within her audience. On one occasion a few years prior, I was within her audience attending an informational seminar. Suzanne was amazing, and I became very engrossed as she spoke. After some time, I became one of the lucky ones along with my mother to have received a heavenly message. We both had complete validation that day as she told us things pertaining to our deceased loved ones in a very healing manner. Upon another occasion, Suzanne correctly connected me to my grandmother. And her message was for Joey,(who was very much alive at this time.) She mentioned being with him and very proud of his accomplishments. The unique delivery and precision of her words could in no way have ever been fabricated. There was so much detail and the names she addressed them as, were very accurate.

Today that seemed so long ago, but I felt that this, and my faith in God was a good direction to begin while gathering some strength. I had to begin to help my shattered heart, at least this way I would know my son was okay. Soon my eyes became so heavy, and I drifted off to sleep.

The following morning, after catching approximately an hour or so of light sleep, all of the family was up again. One of my daughters, Gabrielle, was loudly calling for me from the other room she had slept in. I didn't really want to move, but my motherly instinct slammed me into protection mode! Little did I know then how Joey already had begun to fulfill his devoted promise. As soon as I entered the room, she began rambling on about Joey. I had to stop and clear my mind while trying to offer her all of my attention, that I could gather. She began to describe an almost unbelievable vivid dream.

Gabrielle said that in her dream, Joey came to her wearing a green sweater with a red stripe across the chest. He was also wearing a beige pair of pants. (This was an outfit he wore often.) He also had his wallet in the side pocket of his pants. He was telling her something about a note. Now Gabrielle was still very young, and she hadn't known anything about a note. Her sister Isabelle secretly had placed a note in his wallet earlier that evening; its contents were filled with love for her brother. (Obviously they do receive our messages.) This seemed to be his unexpected way of replying to us all for the first time. Gabrielle recalled within the dream how Joey came to her and told her he would watch over her and sleep with her that night. Gabrielle had always leaned on her big brother a little more than her sisters. He had definitely become her idol throughout the years. This was especially true, because of the difficulties she faced after her birth. Joey had remained as a great influence in her young life. She needed him especially now, but he could not help her in the same manner as he always had.

She described to us how, within her dream, she even felt his arms around her, which is exactly how he comforted her many times in the past. She went on to describe the dream, saying, "Mom, he slept at my head. He told me to tell you to stop crying."

He also appeared to another sister, Gianna, in a dream that very same night. He told her he was happy and also to tell everyone to stop crying. All I could imagine was, he must feel our overwhelming pain and grief. This encounter did offer some relief as I anticipated, but that was of little consolation at the time. That request from Joey in both his sister's dream was a lot easier said than done. I imagined I would probably cry for the rest of my life. I kept thinking I will never ever get through this. Never again wanting to return to the many burdens of life. Instead my internal wish was to refuse to pick up the fragmented pieces and continue. It all seemed so incredibly hard. If only I could stop the world from revolving, so I could escape from dealing with all the ramifications that are yet to come. I was soon to discover that the death of a child seems to be attached to a deeply driven common thread of suffering. I believe parents including myself share a great fear their child would slowly become only a name filled with great pain, a name that will surely be forgotten as time continued to proceed until one day, when it completely will dissipate. Then our deceased loved one's name to forever remain only uttered in a whisper, as if it has become some sort of taboo.

My promise to Joey would be to never let that happen. Our continual bond of love will always be acknowledged. His name will never become overlooked or feared to be spoken in our home or anywhere else. His essence will linger within our lives forever.

As days went by I tried to grasp some strength, so I turned further to a salvation I always held dear: my faith in God. I visited the very church I was married in. My children were also baptized there. I began to recite the rosary daily and sent all prayers for my Joey. Many times my children would join me. My bargaining with God had begun. I begged and pleaded to somehow see my son!

I also continued to be consumed with life-after-death books. I was searching for more to aid my continual bleeding heart. Many books repeat a lot of the same important details: that there is a continuation of life and you will see your loved one again. As this helped in reassurance, I was searching and I needed much more. The book that really helped me at this point was by George Anderson, *Walking in the Garden of Souls*. The words really hit home. It began to pave a narrow path toward something to hold on to. I was still attempting to fill the uncertainty that resided within me. Soon that book went with me everywhere within my home. Every chance I got, my eyes were glued to the pages. It helped me through many tough days but most importantly through the long, dark, grief-stricken nights. These nights were when I chose to be alone with my pain. This was the hardest because I would not and could not add to my children's pain or my husband's. I especially didn't want my daughters to see a continually broken mother. I even felt like I had to be a firm anchor for my husband, who was completely inconsolable. As I began absorbing the book deeply, it had resurrected a sense of buried familiarity to it. Something was being awakened deep in my soul, which somehow had been long forgotten. I desperately needed to have a firm grip of what would later become a validated hope to weather this hard wave of life ahead of us all.

Once I had completed reading George Anderson's book, I felt a temporary sense of minute relief, so then I wanted even more. On my search, I then came across a book containing signs our loved ones send from the other side, which was also a great help to me. The book was titled; *Hello from Heaven* by Bill and Judy Guggenheim. Soon I was consumed with looking for signs everywhere, and believe me; many are there once you draw your attention to them. The book described the way signs would come to you from a loved one who had crossed over. I learned that the signs came in a variety of ways, ranging from subtle to the very dramatic. This book also made reference to dream visitation as did the previous books. There were descriptions of how signs could easily be disregarded because most would not be immediately noticed unless you heighten your awareness. It mentioned how a bereaved family member usually becomes absorbed within a state of despondency and despair. You had to find a new way to become aware and to learn a kind of foreign language or else it's dismissed as only hopeful thinking. When you begin to notice them over and over, they have the power to heal. These, along with a few other dreams that had occurred for others, helped me to really start believing our family remains connected to us after death. They want us to know they are safe and sound and free of all the worries and hardships of the earth, we still face. Our pain must be felt by them on some level; that must be why such comfort is sent. I do assume they send it the best way it will be received by us and will be most helpful.

I began to slowly build a little security knowing my son is in heaven and hold onto my belief that it is wonderful by the many near-death stories I have read about. Yet my motherly instinct wants to have some sense of control over the situation. That I don't have, and it is a scary and a very unfamiliar feeling. At times when I still can't help it, I do slip into a helpless and overwhelming deep, dark hole. I can't and don't want to remain in that place, so I will continue my search for real salvation, a search for the only thing that can rescue me, the love of my son. I would soon learn how powerful love was. More than I could have ever imagined. Proof of his promise to remain forever with us would soon become evident. As developments unfolded, his devotion became much more than anything I could have ever hoped for.

CHAPTER 5

A STRENGTH UNLEASHED

The power of love cannot be contained
We are bound to each other
With heavenly strength and courage
Baby steps initiate a growing aluminous transformation
How deeply we love
Is not measured by the depth of our fall
Or the duration of our indebted despondency
It is, however, when you continue to survive
Faced with the almighty fears of life once again
You prove the bonds of love
Reach beyond the barriers of our comprehension
And are never ending.

The Marianne I once was had now become a stranger to me. Somehow I had faded within this hollow shell, I had unwillingly become. My days progressed as if I was now some robotic zombie carrying on with only the basic and necessary daily obligations. My world and life were completely shattered. I found my will and my once-powerful strength within me, completely gone.

As time went on, many days of deep despair resurfaced over and over again. I had unfortunately descended into the bottomless and very dark isolated hole. It seemed as though life would never resume with an ability to survive. Every passing minute quickly became a blur into nothingness. It was as if I could not see anything beyond my pain.

Unknowingly, a small sense of comfort emerged from an unlikely source, unbelievably from our new dog named Lucky. The dog that at one time I didn't want! We had found Lucky one month prior to Joey's crossing at a local dog pound.(I soon realized the name was perfect, because we were just as lucky to have found him as he was to find us.) Often Lucky snuggled up to me while emanating a sense of compassion and companionship. I loved the comfort my dog brought to me. As I reflect on this thought, I realize he truly seemed to recognize my deep despair. As days went on, he instinctively clung to my side more often. This occurred mostly during my times of loneliness when my husband had returned to work and my children were back at school. His affection felt like a minibandage attempting to aide my huge gaping wound.

Regardless, like a timid child, I continued to shut myself out from the world. This broken person was so unlike my true self as I was afraid of what people thought and of the whispers that I may overhear. I thought to myself, *how will I handle a conversation with someone? What if they are inquisitive and ask questions that I simply could not handle?* My fear intensified and had grown to become overwhelmingly very powerful. I knew I would crumble, as I constantly feared what my ears would hear. I knew I needed to protect my heart somehow as best as I could. So I avoided everything that may compound my excruciating pain. I was thrown into such chaos while trying to carry a monumental weight, which had an impact on everything. Even the simplest tasks sent a wave of fear through me. It's a shame how some people do become oblivious as to what type of impact their words may have on a grieving individual. This fear had grown into a monster, and it was continually hard to contain.

Remember, unless you have been in the shoes of another's circumstance, you will never understand. There is no possible way of understanding this level of loss or the effect it has. What may seem obvious to you regarding a person's feelings may actually be totally off base. Just because visibly someone may look okay do not conclude that they are. To be most helpful is to speak always with kindness and continue to tread lightly. Always choose your words carefully so they may be received in a healing way. Put yourself clearly second and this person's fragile state first. No matter how much time has elapsed. You simply cannot put your time frame on someone else's pain.

With this new realization, I thought back to the many past tragedies shown within the evening news on television. As the events were described, I listened and of course felt bad. But now I can unfortunately say, I truly empathize with them on some recognizable level. As I stated before, I am not going to kid myself. My understanding is found within my circumstance alone. Certainly everyone is not faced with the monumental tragedy due to the loss of a child. Loss comes in many forms. Throughout our lives though, we all must face it within some capacity. Realistically there isn't a home that will remain completely untouched.

Slowly, I really began my understanding of how much of my life would be affected. Everyday functions continued to take a great deal of courage. Everywhere I went, there was still no escaping; daily reminders are always there. Somehow though, life goes on, so sooner or later I must also.

Within life, there are many occasions that once we so longed for, however now, they are faced with reluctance while maintaining a level of fear. Birthdays, graduations, weddings, births, etc., had become a monumental feat. Joining these celebrations increasingly grew *very* difficult. It had nothing to do with jealousy; it's because of the constant reminder of your deepest pain. Lost occasions become haunting and inescapable. This recognition had now become a double-edged sword. You are happy for them, but you can't help from thinking of yourself. And I find that a lot of people just don't understand this. It swallows you up among past longings you once had toward celebrations, but now you know you will never see.

As I thought I would completely not want to take another step in this so-called life I found myself in, something began to stir in me slowly. A buried strength somehow had started to awaken. I thought of the people that I had recently met. They had gone out of their way to visit and share their own stories of loss. It was an attempt to extend themselves in a supportive way. Many of the stories were comforting, but the few that stuck in my mind most were the ones where people lost all hope. Even though a great amount of years had passed since their loss, they still seemed to be so grief stricken and separated completely from life. It revealed to me a possibility of an unrelenting and very bleak future for the rest of our lives. Is that what is in store for me and my family's future? To forever remain where we are and refuse to ever budge again? To live among loved ones segregated, never to be included within any kind of family unity again, while each one of us faced a battle of our own? I realized this was not a healthy way to live. As I had these thoughts running through my mind, I tried to concentrate on the circumstances and weigh out the probable outcomes. Slowly I concluded that if I did not choose to join life again, it *will* move right along without me anyways, probably in a direction that was not of the best of outcomes.

While knowing our family will have a very difficult and long road, we must strive to support each other and try to slowly pick up the pieces. We need to cautiously press forward and wait for some kind of normalcy to return one day. While our gradual healing is a focused goal, hope must remain on the horizon. I do not want us to remain through life so weak, it eventually divides us permanently.

The thought that kept rushing through my mind was how would Joey want me to handle this? He had such incredible strength and courage in all that he ever did in life. Do I want to remain in that black hole forever paralyzed? Or to be the mother I always was for my children and the mother I have to become again with hopefully a newfound strength I can muster over time, which at some point should help to lighten the incredible weight my whole family must now carry? I focused and began to fill myself with the thoughts of Joey and how he was and still is a big part of our lives.

I made a bargain within myself and vowed to continually try to gather this hope-filled strength. Then somehow we can weather this enormous storm. While we all can never forget our Joey, we must try to focus on his strength and love he so freely shared. I will use all of my being to squeeze them tight within my heart's grasp forever. Throughout time, I will maintain a new focus on retaining our memories while continuing to try taking each day one at a time. I reminded myself to forge ahead at a slow but steady and even keel. Every few days, I tried to push myself a pinch forward more, attempting tiny baby steps. (For some just by getting out of bed is a step toward survival.) When the phone rang, instead of always freezing, I would more often find the courage to answer it. After I mastered that challenge, I tried to move onto another. My next step became a short trip to the store.

As I attempted to venture out though, I must admit it took me a while before I attempted that alone. I typically would arm myself with a relative by my side. I knew I was more than this. I would continue to remind myself that if I continued to crumble, so would my family. I realized my key focus must always remain on the love we still continue to share for strength. I was always reasoning within myself. I knew I could also count on God, and of course on my Joey! He was a very strong young man, and I would not and could not let him down. In time, I'm sure my healing will become steadier with the love I receive from my son on a daily basis. This energizing love is welcoming and soothing to my soul and continually strengthens my faith. A faith, once ignited, continues to brighten as a beacon of hope I wish to embrace forever within me.

I know there will still be many days where I will fall upon my knees as the reality of the situation consumes and continually challenges me. I will not fool myself. I believe now I have come to the fact, that is to be expected. My conceded philosophy became this: there are many pieces to the puzzle of life; this piece was the heaviest one. However, there are many lighter and wonderful pieces. My hope is that in the end, when it is all put together, there is some logical reason for people such as us to suffer such monumental loss.

Through our family tragedy, we gained many new friends. As I have said, people who are in similar circumstances, do seem to understand on a much deeper level. They recognize the effect it has on you and also the uphill battle ahead. I really feel anyone who steps forward to help another is a selfless act. It was like they were tapping into a reserve of unconditional love while still grieving for themselves. No one can comprehend the magnitude of such a pain as this, unless you are also a bereaved parent.

We became very drawn to a particular family who had gone through the devastation of losing a child, not that long before. This child also had so much promise along with many accomplishments throughout his short life. Unfortunately, they surely recognized our heartbreak. Still they found the strength to come visit us and offer us their support. My husband and I were profoundly touched by this kindness. They had found a way to survive and had attempted to extend their strength to us. Soon after their initial visit, we began seeing more and more of them and we eventually became good friends.

There seemed to be an unspoken language of consideration and compassion between us. Encouragement at this time had meant so much from them. To be in contact with a family that has endured tragedy similar to ours and yet still functioning was promising. This alone offered us great hope. We felt a strong desire to follow their lead. The friendship strengthened us, and it continued to grow over time. Anytime the subject of survival after death came up, we would discuss it openly. We all shared the knowledge we had gained through our experience. Most of all we believed through our faith, we would someday see our children again.

My husband and this neighbor had an especially tight brotherhood bond. Soon, it would seem that they had become inseparable. They found in each other a shared void as fathers who have both lost their only sons. We wives would tease them because sometimes we felt a little left out. As time progressed, these blossoming friendships continued to help tremendously. I thank this friend especially for helping my husband to cope. I knew the next hurdle would be to accept all that has happened. It would take a great deal of courage, and I knew it was a step that must be taken somehow. I needed to maintain a faith that the separation to our children residing in heaven, is temporary. This belief had more and more become very important. I hold tight to the hope that one day our deep wounds of pain shall be healed.

FAITH

I have never left you
I have merely shed my earthly body and now exist within
my heavenly one
I am forever a part of you as you are of me
Remember, love lingers
Beckon me within your thoughts and I hear you
Call out my name and somehow I will answer within a
heavenly sign
My sign however may be subtle, but rest assured we are
forever connected
Open a receptive heart for me
Trust everything has a meaning
One day you shall join me to share heavenly bliss blessed
with our eternal...
L O V E

CHAPTER 6

OUT OF THE MOUTHS OF BABES

Listen to your children, their innocence speaks volumes.

Approximately three days after Joey's funeral, my daughters—Gianna, age nine; Lynn, age thirteen—and their cousin Susan, age twelve, were in a downstairs room together. They were talking among themselves when Gianna suddenly became startled. She stood up and walked over toward the hallway. Then to their shock, she said, "Joey?" They looked at her like she was crazy.

They said, "What are you saying, Gianna? You're freaking us out!"

Just then she proceeded through the hallway and entered the furnace room. Gianna then turned to the others, who had quickly followed her. She said, "I just saw Joey walking in this hallway, then into this room!"

Clearly they really hadn't expected to hear that, so they were all unsure of just how to react. They all looked at each other for answers. Our family was of course, very emotional at this early period of our grief. So, I'm sure the first thought they all had was since they have been through so much pain, their imagination now has gone a bit haywire.

Gianna's older sister, Lynn, nervously tried to lighten the intense situation with an attempt at a little humor. "Well then," she said, "let me wear his chain you're wearing, and I might see him too. Maybe there's something special about it."

So Gianna, clearly still stunned, didn't argue. She just handed over the chain as she still stood in her confused state. Lynn put it on and had no reaction, so obviously she was unable to see him.

Then somehow Gianna intuitively knew she should check the next room, which was appropriately Joey's bedroom. As she looked, she instantly saw him sitting on his workout bench!

He said, "Hi, Gianna!"

She turned to the other girls and said, "Don't you see him? He just said hi to me!"

Susan and then Lynn said, "No."

At this point they ran out of the room and were calling for me. "Mom!"

"Auntie Marianne!"

I came running downstairs into the room where they were. Then Gianna told me about Joey's appearance. At first I thought, she is missing her brother so much, she's pretending. Then she persisted in telling me what she saw. She was so convincing as she went on describing each and every detail of the experience. My heart soared. I thought I should pinch myself to be sure I wasn't dreaming. We all have been through a lot. Internally though, I already knew this was possible. I suppose I also feared, at the same time, if it wasn't true, it would further upset all of us. I stopped myself and thought it through again.

I said to her, "Are you sure, Gianna?"

"Yes, Mom, I wouldn't make up something like that," Gianna said.

Everyone was in shock as we were trying to absorb this monumental event. A short time later, Gianna looked out to the backyard. She said, "Now he's leaning against the lower half of the deck. And he is smiling, Mom. He looks very happy!"

Little did I know this was the beginning of a never-ending communication that would continue to be delivered to us! I felt that this was truly a miracle. However, I later would learn this is not so uncommon, especially among family members. The only sense I now can make of this is that there must be some plan in life for all of us to fulfill. And we clearly are here now to help each other while carrying out our roles. Joey and his sister must have made a vow to keep this heavenly connection to benefit us and many others.

Approximately two days later, Joey visited Gianna again. This time, however, it was in school while she was seated during gym class. Quickly she somehow knew how to play it off, so she wouldn't bring attention to herself while in the company of others. Joey appeared and told her as gentle as possible that his time had come to enter heaven and that he loved her very much. He then seemed to try to extend further help. "Please tell Mom and Dad to stop crying. There are a lot of people who know them here."

Then something else wonderful happened. He began to show her what seemed like a vision. However, this vision, as she later explained, was somehow within her own mind. As it began to unfold, she was shown a different place, which she thought must be heaven. Joey quickly confirmed this thought with assurance of its beauty! Gianna was then amazed as she saw exquisite flowers. Everything appeared to be much brighter as they were encompassed within an immense light. The images were hard for her to comprehend; somehow they were magnified.

That day, many other heavenly visions were delivered to Gianna. This removed any question of its validity. Joey then told her and showed her how he was in the company of angels. They seemed to be childlike angels; they were amusing each other.

He then informed her that all the animals we had owned on earth and had passed away, were with him! He then smiled and said, "Let's always keep this connection."

She eagerly confirmed his request and said, "Yeah, let's always keep this connection!"

That afternoon, when she arrived home from school, she couldn't wait to tell me all that had transpired. She spoke as if it was a normal conversation between her and her brother. It was a great comfort to her. As she told me, I was completely in awe; I didn't know how to react. It was so much to absorb! I felt like pinching myself again to be sure I wasn't dreaming. From that point on, I knew what she had explained was real. I recalled having some of my own experiences as a child; I will explain one instance in another chapter.

Throughout my life, I had always remained interested in the afterlife subject. My faith and other experiences kept my belief, but I never could have imagined all of these convincing experiences. Later that night, I entered Gianna and Gabrielle's bedroom. Surprisingly their brother still had plenty more to say. As I entered the room, Gianna said, "Mom, Joey was just here. He left when you opened the door."

"Oh," I said, taken a little off guard. I thought a minute for the proper reaction. Quickly I spoke up so I didn't upset them. "Then I will go out so you can speak to him." I returned to the kitchen and attempted to prepare supper as my thoughts rushed by. I asked myself how I can possibly attempt to cook while feeling as if my head may explode with joy at any moment! I was trying to contain my excitement and stay busy until they were finished, but it was very hard. I anticipated how I would retain every last detail of this latest experience. I also wanted to tend to their tender feelings of loss at the same time.

Shortly, the two sisters emerged from the room. They both had huge beaming smiles on their faces. They didn't seem upset as they proceeded down the hallway to the kitchen where I stood.

Gianna said, "Joey is standing right here!" Suddenly they both had a surprised look on their faces after a glance toward each other. "Mom, he just disappeared." Then instinctively Gianna made a comment in an attempt to comfort me. "Mom, he must have been needed in heaven."

I clearly disguised my internal reaction as you might have guessed. I didn't want to upset them or make Gianna feel afraid of upsetting me. It was clear Joey was now in the role of a teacher or parent. The previous roles between us were reversed. I knew I needed to trust him since now he had all the facts and I didn't.

These visits soon became very frequent. Never did two or more days pass without a Joey visit. The following night, Gianna and

Gabrielle were talking while sitting on their bed. I entered the room to kiss them good night.

Gianna said, "Mom, Joey is here with us. He is sitting on the bed." So I leaned in close. Then she said to me, "Mom, he's hugging you right now."

I took full advantage of this opportunity while trying to keep my composer. I stopped and took a deep breath and tried to comprehend this great leap of love. My heart so needed all I was receiving. I next uttered the words, "Tell him I love him."

"He says he loves you too, Mom," Gianna said. At that moment, I found myself becoming very overwhelmed, so I became silent. Then Gianna said, "Joey told me he loves me and Gabrielle very much." To receive these words from Joey was so reassuring, but I also had deep, unanswered questions screaming within me for answers at the same time. I had to clearly use caution while needing this information. As delicately as I could, while containing my composure at the same time, I searched within me for questions to ask. Immediately, a question quickly rushed to my lips. "Gianna, ask him if there is anything I could have changed that day to keep him here on earth?"

"No, Mom. Joey said it was his time."

"Did you suffer?" I quickly and directly asked next.

"No," he said firmly through Gianna.

As a parent, these were the two most haunting questions I carried with me. I desperately needed them answered, and Gianna answered them as if she was much older than her age. Some nights I would jolt up in bed, my mind would race with all the possibilities. All of them shook me to the core. I had constantly wondered if I had somehow let him down. That just maybe I didn't fulfill my role as a protecting parent enough. It is a cruel but all too often true suffering no parent should have to experience. It is something that cannot be undone, and I believe I will carry that thought for the rest of my life. However, now I needed to find my composure and not get carried away with my questions. I needed to keep in mind that we were all suffering this great sense of grief, and these questions packed a heavy wallop. Joey must have known this because he stayed a little longer, then told Gianna it was time for him to return. Just like that, he was gone.

After some time, my curiosity pushed me to make a few other inquiries. I asked Gianna, "What did he look like? What was he wearing?" She said, "He looks like my brother, Mom. How he always looked." (I don't know what I expected for her reply.) "The only difference now is usually he appears dressed in white. Oh, Mom, also he has white lines coming from all around him."

I really didn't know what to make of this. But I somehow knew it was all true. There is no way my daughter would ever think something like this up. I would have never expected the kind of description she gave me. My daughter, even though a child, was proving to me that the bonds of love are forever.

One day in particular, Gianna had not heard from Joey. So she walked outside and took it upon herself to try and call him. Where she had come up with this knowledge, I don't know. Once outside, Gianna closed her eyes and mentally called to her brother. He didn't appear; however, something much unexpected happened.

As soon as Gianna returned inside, she said, "Mom, I tried to reach Joey. And instead, a very nice woman came. She said, "Your brother cannot speak to you right now, but he will always be with you." Gianna was surely surprised. Her eyes were wide, full of wonder and excitement as she spoke. "She was beautiful, Mom. She had a white shawl over her head, and she was covered in blue clothing."

As my mind tried to grasp the information my ears were hearing, a sudden rush of goose bumps ran through my body. I was suddenly filled with emotion and complete shock. I tried to collect some composure so that I wouldn't frighten Gianna. I took her by the hand, walked her into my bedroom, and opened my bureau drawer. I quickly reached in and pulled out a copy of a painting my aunt had done long ago. She is a very gifted and intuitive artist. The painting was of the Virgin Mary. At the time of creating the painting, she merely followed her impressions, without any prompting from a photograph. Gianna had never seen this painting copy, so I showed it to her. She immediately replied, "Mom, that's her!" I remember my knees getting very weak and wobbly. I guess I still was in a little disbelief of the possibility of something so astounding occurring. I stood in silence for a moment as I tried to comprehend this latest revelation. I kept thinking, *Can this be real?* How can we be so honored and blessed to receive such a visit? While we were in our small little world, how can it be possible for us to have an important individual role? A simple explanation must be, as many of us feel unrecognized, the truth is we really aren't. We all have an important role in God's plan. Although, it does at times seem difficult to fully understand.

As all these happenings were quite comforting, they still didn't remove the reality of the pain, which is still very much attached to the physical loss of our precious Joey. Just to continue to function was still very difficult. Over and over, the daily reminders were always there to face and challenge me. They were everywhere I went. Many moments of grief seemed to hit me out of the blue.

While many times I was so overwhelmed with my own pain, I knew I needed to always remember Gianna was also grieving. So I listened and allowed her to speak as often as she needed to. I comforted my daughter in the best way I could. She would share the many happenings with me, and I would always give her my full attention. I attempted to explain as best I could with the little I had known while acknowledging the miracle we were all experiencing.

As wonderful as all this was, still she was a child and enjoyed what most children her age do. Spending time playing in the yard was still a favorite of Gianna's along with her sister, Gabrielle. Frequently they would ride while sitting upon skateboards up and down the driveway. They have a great bond of love and enjoyed each other's company very much. Heavenly visits developed often on many of these outside activities.

On one occasion, a neighbor's two children were playing in their nearby yard. Gianna and her sister were also outside and walked over to visit, since they were friends.

One of the children was very young, about two years old. My girls made a special fuss over her because she was so cute and playful. They would join in on the fun helping the older sister entertain her. They all enjoyed laughing and hovering over the younger girl as little mother hens. This afternoon, Gianna looked up to the sky and was overjoyed to see Joey's face smiling back at her. To her surprise, she glanced over, and this very young child was waving to him! Joey waved back. Gianna was completely shocked that she was not the only one who could see him. She just watched as this young child's full attention was on Joey, but she did not let on to the others.

This proves children are very open to the other side. Parents who have lost children may receive visits through younger family members. Just maybe, that so-called imaginary friend they refer to actually may not be so imaginary. It was clear; Gianna had now developed a system enabling her to reach her brother. Always she would start with a prayer. Then mentally she would think of him, calling to his spirit. Almost every time, this worked.

It was a few weeks after Joey's passing, and visits were still occurring, but not quite as frequently. So she began to use this new system if a few days went by without receiving such a visit. She very much wanted to hear from him and expected him to show. As she attempted this connection, she was surprised again when someone different showed up. A new heavenly visitor appeared as a little girl who also had lines of white light coming from her. She spoke to Gianna also and informed her, that she was a working angel messenger for Joey. She said her name was Jessica and Joey could not visit now because he was busy in heaven. Jessica did not explain just what he was busy with, but somehow Gianna knew it was important. She told Gianna that Joey was loved by everyone there and he was very nice.

Shortly after this, still another little angel girl visited her. Her name was Haley; soon she and Jessica became Gianna's spiritual friends. Many times, when Joey didn't show up, one of them usually did. They offered hope and encouragement to her whichever way she may have needed it at the time. I searched within my mind for an explanation for their appearance. I thought maybe appearing as children was easier for Gianna to handle and communicate with, when her brother was unavailable.

A few weeks later one day, the girls and I went for a ride to get out of the house. We decided to visit a nearby farm and bring carrots as a special treat to feed the horses. On our way, we made sure to stop for a visit at the church. A little peace was found for us there, so each time we were out it had quickly become as a ritual to stop. Once we had arrived, we always prayed, knowing prayer was a wonderful gift of love to offer our Joey. We were also, of course, hoping for him to visit us. Upon our entering the church that day, we walked over to light a candle. Once lit, we all sat down for our individual prayers. As we all began to pray, it seemed Gianna began speaking to someone, which of course we immediately figured was a spiritual visitor. We were now becoming a little more comfortable with these startling occurrences.

Then Gianna began describing to me all she was seeing and referred to this vision as another angel visitor. This angel spoke to Gianna and said, "Your brother cannot be here right now, but he will meet you when you visit the horse farm."

Gianna's quick response was, "How do you know we are going there?"

The angel answered her by saying, "We see everything."

Gianna replied matter-of-factly with, "Oh, okay." Obviously even with her reply, she was still a little confused, but she accepted it and never doubted a word. Then she told us the angel seemed to float upward and disappear. Occurrences seemed so natural now with Gianna's new created attitude toward them. We all were beginning to learn to accept these visits in stride along with her.

When we arrived at the horse farm, we prepared to feed the horses. As the horses noticed the carrots that were dangled by the girls, they quickly approached us and gobbled them up. When all the carrots were gone and the girls finished petting them, we walked over to the car. Gianna then said, "Joey is over there with the horses, Mom."

He then said to her, "Hey, Gianna, I thought you knew everything about horses." He knew how she had always collected posters and calendars filled with horses on them. She had also read many books about the caring of them. So her response quickly broke into laughter as she called him over to us. As he approached us, I was swift to take advantage and asked for a kiss. Gianna said, "He's doing that right now, Mom."

I said, "We all love you and miss you, Joey."

He said, "I love and miss you too, but I'm right here!"

Then I continued, "I miss us watching television together, and I miss hugging you."

He returned with, "I know, but I am always nearby."

I next asked, "Will Gianna always be able to see you?"

"Yes," he replied.

Next I asked, "Do you receive my prayers?"

"Yes, in a special way" he said. (I had been saying the rosary daily for him.)

Then, I couldn't help myself I needed to ask, "Could I have changed anything to keep you here?"

"No," he said. "It was my time, Mom. Tell Dad not to cry and suffer so much."

Soon after that, he said good-bye and was no longer seen by Gianna. This latest visit was so precious and healing to us, yet there was still so much more to come.

On Sundays, the girls and I began attending mass regularly. We always felt better as we prayed and continued the practice of lighting candles for Joey once the mass was over. Upon our first visit together, Gianna realized how our prayers are truly heard. People held hands as the Lord's Prayer was said out loud, by all. This time, however, Gianna led our attention to the person who was at the end of the pew. He appeared not to be holding anyone's hand; she informed us that in actuality, it was not the case. Angels appeared and held the empty hand of each person at the end of each pew.

Upon our future visits, Joey appeared also and many times spoke to Gianna. We found it difficult to always remain quiet. We greatly appreciated the peace we received while in God's house and we became very enthusiastic. Anticipation always grew prior to Sunday mass to hear of Gianna's experience. With each visit, as soon as it was time for the Lord's Prayer, all our eyes would be fixed on her. As it continually occurred during each Mass, we realized how very powerful this prayer is. Each visit afterward strengthened this faith. Truly, *we are always heard.*

A few Sundays later, there was still another amazing visit. We began to pray, and Gianna revealed to us a vision as it unfolded. She said an angel appeared in front of her sister, Gabrielle, who was seated next to her. She began to explain the vision to her. Then for some reason, I felt that this messenger was assisting in Gabrielle's healing. (She was now at a crossroad in meeting her educational needs. When Joey was still alive, he had always encouraged her, and now it seemed he was offering her further help.) This angel, unrecognized by Gianna, reached out and touched her sister's face. All of a sudden, Gianna saw that Joey had also appeared in front of them. He smiled when she noticed him. Then he pressed his fingers together and opened them, directed at Gabrielle's forehead. It appeared to Gianna as if he was sending something from within his spiritual fingers. She described the motion as if flicking water off your fingers towards someone.

He also had huge wings that Gianna noticed. Now, I'm not trying to say that he is an angel. It is said by many that angels do not incarnate as humans; only God knows the truth in that. I have read though, where an angel can incarnate for a short time while delivering guidance and offering protection; Joey clearly did both. Most likely though, it was an attempt for us to understand he was assisting in delivering Gabrielle heavenly help. For whatever the reason may actually be really doesn't matter. I will never have all the answers while I am on earth, and that will have to suffice. This is just the way he chose to show himself at this time. Again it makes a lot of sense, especially as a further symbolic explanation. It seemed to help us understand the level of healing he was able to deliver and just how evolved he was. I suppose it may point out the work he continues doing, in heaven.

After Gianna told us all she had seen, she then curiously asked him, "What are you doing, Joey?"

His only response was, "You'll see."

I believe he continues watching over his sister as he always did in life. This thought was soon confirmed by Gianna.

PHOTOS

This is the stone located at the entrance of the high school football field. It was painted purple and surrounded by white stones, which represented the school football uniform colors. This was done days after Joey's crossing, as a memorial.

This plaque was recently placed upon the purple "Stone" in Joey's memory, eleven years after his crossing.

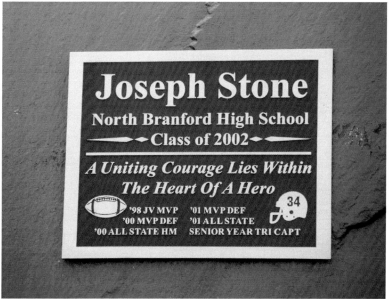

I wrote this statement as I was divinely guided.

This is the road named after Joey.

My husband and I, along side of Joey on Senior night.

Here's Joey lined up just prior to a football game. His Tarzan roar was always released, following the National Anthem.

Joey and his father embracing after a game.

Joey's class photo.

Joseph Nicholas Stone

The press box at the high school football field was decorated by grieving friends and classmates of Joey's.

A close-up photo of the decorated football press box.

The back of the high school field press box, decorated by Joey's friends and classmates, with love.

This is the angel I noticed right outside my
front door, after I completed my book.

The angel slowly floats over our home.

A closeup view.

The angel slowly dissipates as it began to rise upward.

Eleven years after Joey's crossing, yet another angel cloud
formation appeared while out shopping with Marti.

While vacationing with Marti and friends on a popular beach in
Maine, I took many photos. Most photos were filled with orbs,
but this one stood out for it had something extra special. I see
my Joey's face posing with his hands beneath his chin. (I happen
to have a photo of him in the same pose at home.) You can also
see an appearance of the Virgin Mary in the lower left corner.

My photo while attending an Energy Healing
workshop. I was reassured Joey was with me,by the huge
orb beside my knee.(Orbs represent spiritual presence.)

CHAPTER 7

THE SECRET

Something delivered to you that is
so special and so precious
Your heart soars with exhilaration,
yet it must remain contained
Upon release, it can change lives
Once believed, it inspires
Yet it may be somewhat misunderstood for now
When the time is right, all will be revealed
And send healing to all who search for it.

As all of Gianna's visits continued to occur, the wave of comfort
it brought offered a brief sense of euphoria! I wanted to scream
it from the rooftops, but I knew I couldn't. People would think I
was completely nuts! Yet within me, I wished somehow this secret
could be revealed to help people hold on to their hope and find the
same comfort. But for now, we would all be sworn to secrecy. Could
you imagine the school's child psychologist? My girls would be put
in straightjackets. I was also afraid people would try to convince
Gianna it wasn't possible. The result may squash the faith within
her, while stifling her abilities. So we all agreed not to draw attention, especially while spirit was present.

I wanted to remember all that was occurring, every last detail.
There was just too much to absorb, so I began to keep a journal. I

felt like I had been hoarding a great secret that someday may be shared with all who search for it. I also felt it was another way I could honor my son. I think maybe Gianna was seeing Joey so this book could be created, to ignite hope in people.

Strength continually was found within all the visits, along with the love my family shared, and of course my Joey. And while I valued the relief Gianna's messages had offered me, I still desired more. That was when I truly realized how one can transcend to becoming empowered to survive. So I must reveal another source of my finding strength. I met a great psychic medium, which is also a wonderful healer.

Her name is Marti, and she offers healing messages from deceased loved ones on the other side. Her earliest messages were delivered in person and over the phone. I credit her with reinforcing much of my acquired strength to understand all that was transpiring. Marti has a sweet and healing voice. When she speaks, an immediate sense of calmness soothes and consoles you. Then a welcoming and overwhelming wave of love consumes you. You could just feel the love that outwardly radiated from within her. There was no doubt; the words she spoke were surely heaven sent.

Marti has a special ingredient and level of compassion that helped support my newfound and sustaining hope. This wave of hope, I discovered, is a tool to cherish for life. It's almost as if she had a hidden treasure chest within her grasp filled with specific tools geared for a grieving person's specific need. Each tool was wrapped with compassion, inspiration, validation, and a healthy dose of healing. All were delivered through heavenly messages with the best of intentions and without a shred of selfishness. The messages she delivered were simply undeniable and precise, something that my broken heart so longed to hear and validate.

Marti's messages were so validating because she was not connected to our family in any way. Her messages were confirming that my son was still very much a part of our lives and this ignited our further belief. As she relayed messages from Joey, she truly had an ability to capture his personality, which we immediately recognized.

The many messages I received through Marti had the ability to reach deep within my heart. The result was resurfacing much more of my forgotten strength for survival. The most important thing I learned was, I was stronger than I had realized and I would be able to weather this great storm in life. If I could continue to keep a firm grip on hope, I would stay strong and then maybe all of my family would regain a sense of security again. Hopefully one day we would be able to successfully handle the fear that comes with rejoining all of the many obstacles in life.

I began to realize that the days and nights that were once only filled with despair and hopelessness had now really gained momentum towards change. Some sense of joy was slowly finding a way to spill into our family again. As the balance of validations from Marti and Gianna continued, the pieces of this puzzle began to make some sort of sense, even though I know while on earth we will never have all the answers for our suffering.

Marti always remained open to questions and offered guidance whenever possible. She even gave me loving messages to deliver to friends of mine. Many messages I accepted for Joey's friends, which I was careful to deliver so they didn't think I was some kind of nut! But they were all so powerful. Marti also gave us the validation for the healing Joey had delivered to his sister in the church. Joey's message sent through Marti was that in time, the healing Gabrielle received would truly help her with the challenges in life, she was to face.

In another instance, a reading was held in our home for our family. Marti immediately knew and pointed out where the first appearance of Joey to Gianna had been. During the reading, she explained how Joey had come to earth to teach through his many friendships and the connections that he had made. The suddenness of his crossing just prior to graduating high school inspired people to look within their own lives. This message hit many much harder and would remain with them for a long time to come. She also confirmed how he is a helper to those who cross over, especially children, on the other side.

Now, the secret of Gianna's gift could finally be spoken openly to someone outside our family. Over time, we were also secure enough to share our secret to expanded family members. Slowly this trust grew to a few friends including some of Joey's. But I still had to remain careful with whom I chose to share this with. This information proved to them that the bonds of love they once shared, continues even after Joey's passing from this world.

Joey had a close friend named Paul. While growing up, Paul and Joey had shared many experiences and were always there to support each other. They had attended school together for many years. They had also gone to the many athletic games, dances, parties, etc. So it didn't surprise me when Paul was the first of his friends to call me with a detailed description of a recent and very vivid dream.

In his dream, he found himself in the high school where he and Joey had attended. He noticed a person with blonde hair. He of course, thought that it was just an acquaintance and dismissed it until he found himself staring at a familiar face coming toward him. He tried to focus while he was completely shocked by how real it all seemed to be. Clearly, he was stunned to realize it was his good friend Joey, whom he had missed tremendously. As he continued to focus his attention (while still dreaming) his heart began to pound. He noticed Joey seemed very happy, smiling and then Joey came right up close to him. He thought his heart would pound right out of his chest, because he was thinking this couldn't possibly be real.

Then Joey said, "Hi!" And that was it; immediately he woke up sweating and remembering how very real it all seemed. It deeply affected him. He was soon overwhelmed by a sudden resurfacing wave of grief. He still found the dream healing because this strengthened his believe in the afterlife. Although much later, it became apparent why he needed this encounter even more than others.

Paul immediately called me to tell me all that had occurred. I knew right away that it was clearly a heavenly visit. I could barely contain my excitement. Paul explained how he panicked in the dream and woke up. I thought to myself, *How I wish I could have one of these dreams*. To only feel my son in my arms would really be heaven to me. But then I thought that maybe I haven't had such a dream due to the possibility of the resurfacing of my buried grieving pain. I believe that the joy I would feel in the dream would be crushed and would affect me greatly once I woke up, and the realization hit me. It would feel as if I was reliving the shock of the loss once again. Maybe I would crumble, and this would halt the progression of healing I was making, including the rest of the family's. My heart still very much wished for this.

I began to think about this dream over and over to understand the dynamics of it. I wondered how to initiate such a dream. Then I remembered a conversation I had a few years back before Joey's passing. A friend of mine, Dee, described how she had asked for a dream from her deceased father. Her father had crossed over a few years before, but she had especially been missing him. A few days later, a coworker and friend told her about a dream that included Dee's dad. He had told her how he loved his daughter and then went on to deliver other wonderful messages through her. She was completely elated as her friend reiterated these eternal words of love, even though she wasn't the one to actually experience the dream.

I was surprised by how she received this dream. So I thought I would try a little experiment. I would ask my grandmother who had crossed over many years ago, to visit me in a dream. I focused all my thoughts on her and said internally how I would love to receive a dream from her. So when a couple of days passed and still there wasn't a dream for me, I brushed it off and then forgot about it.

A day or so after I prayed for it, Joey told his Auntie Toni about a vivid dream he had had. He said that his great-grandmother (my grandmother and Auntie Toni's mother) came to him. She had told him how much she loved him. Then she went on to describe how proud she was of him and how she was aware of current friendships within his life. Also, she told him that she sees him while he is in school from heaven (amazingly, that is very similar to the message Suzanne Northrop delivered to me years ago, concerning Joey). She hugged him, and he said it was so real. The dream, he said, seemed to last for a long time. However, he couldn't remember every detail.

When I had heard this from him, there was no question that there was something to this. (After Joey's crossing over, he revealed to Gianna that this grandmother, along with others, had greeted him upon his arrival to the other side.)

So when I recall this past happening involving dreams, I shared this with the rest of our family, and when they felt they were ready, anyone who hadn't had a dream as of yet would try it themselves. Soon all of Joey's sisters had their own wonderful, loving, and extremely vivid healing dreams. They were able to ask him questions, such as whether he had suffered or not. The answer was always, "No." He told them how he loved them and that he was always with them. He told them that he had really never left. He also said they will see him again. This was very reassuring to all of us and helped us a step further toward our healing.

Auntie Toni even called me one day to tell me about an encounter of her own. She said she was waking up one morning and was not yet quite fully awake, when she noticed a figure on the side of her bed. She thought her eyes were playing tricks on her because the figure appeared to be Joey. She had really missed and loved him very much! Then all of a sudden before she could move, he kissed her! As soon as she received that kiss, her whole body shook and then felt numb. She explained it as feeling like when you hit your funny bone. She called me right away to tell me, but I think she still was in a little shock.

My mother also had her own experience, approximately 3 months after Joey's crossing to heaven. While she was in her kitchen preparing a meal one day, something from the other side of the room caught her attention.

She focused her eyes as she took a step closer and she began to notice Joey's smiling face! She said he was dressed in a white shirt and athletic shorts. She gasped and quickly shouted, "Joey?" Then he disappeared.

She was in disbelief initially, as she tried to comprehend what she saw. She quickly composed herself and soon realized this was a validation for her. This revelation strengthened what she had already believed possible.

Over the next few months, Paul went on to receive signs from Joey, including more dreams. One specific dream he experienced was the following year, around the month of March. I find this dream important to explain as I jump ahead for a moment and describe each of them leading up to it. It shows how our loved ones in spirit really do watch over us. Paul called me to tell me he received an edition of *Sports Illustrated* magazine. On the cover was the MVP player of the year wearing a football jersey number 34. He was also wearing a chain with the number 34 dangling from it. He commented that the number reminded him of Joey.

A week or so later, he had a dream of Joey; only this time he didn't freak out. He said he was in a beautiful field, and it was there that he had found him. He was aware somehow of an ability to communicate with his deceased friend. Curiosity took over as he asked him if there truly is a heaven. Joey replied with a quick, "yes."

Next Paul asked, "How is it then?"

Joey was quick to reply, "It's great!"

Then Paul felt overwhelmed with emotion while recalling the loss of his best friend. He gave Joey a hug and said how he had been incredibly missing him. Then he said to Joey, "You were my brother."

Joey was quick to respond with, "You are my brother!"

You see, since Paul was an only child and Joey being the only boy in his family, they had built a bond between them as if they were siblings. Paul went on further to ask him, "Do you see me from heaven?"

Joey quickly responded with a little humor and said, "You wouldn't believe the things I see you doing." Paul felt soothed by Joey's familiar and comical response.

Then suddenly, Paul had the thought of bringing Joey to see his dad in the dream. All at once, they were with Paul's dad. His dad at first didn't seem to respond in the dream and acknowledge seeing

Joey. Then Joey said to Paul's dad, "I was with you at the store when you bought the bottle of Pine Sol."

Then Joey said to Paul, "Why aren't you taking care of my mom? I'm taking care of your mom." (Paul's mom had been ill at the time.) Paul felt Joey's deep compassion and understanding. Paul attempted to focus further on Joey, while still feeling caught up in the realness of the dream communication. Paul recalled later, how he didn't want it to end as he desired to hold onto each and every word. Paul suddenly felt completely emotionally consumed and Joey most likely knowing it, then said, "I'm getting tired." He then sat down in the field where they were. Next, he laid down and Paul noticed Joey closing his eyes and then he went to sleep. That's when Paul's alarm clock went off, and it woke him up. Later on that day, Paul mentioned this dream to his dad with great enthusiasm. His dad listened and said, "Wow, I remember buying a bottle of Pine Sol just the other day!"

Paul's mom and dad had also been close to Joey. He spent a lot of time visiting in their home. After Joey's passing, they were both very kind to us. They offered their help with all we needed, and Paul was one of the pallbearers. Upon Joey's first anniversary of his passing, Paul and his parents visited his grave. Paul's mom became very emotional. Joey had meant a lot to all of them. It was April 20th on Easter Sunday. Late that night, Paul's mom suddenly passed away. When Paul called me the next day, I was so upset upon hearing of this latest tragedy. Now Paul had to face yet another deeply devastating loss. I was quick to rush over and offer any help they would need. I instinctively knew Joey was still helping Paul's mom, and now the dream took on a lot of meaning. Not that this dream could have changed anything, because I believe we leave when we are supposed to leave. But it was more of an extension of love and protection from Joey to tell his friend he was on the job.

I brought Gianna to his mom's wake. Something I normally would not have done. She really wanted to go, so my husband and I brought her along. Once in line for the viewing, Gianna was soon taking Paul aside. Later she told me that his mom was standing there, dressed in all white. She was extremely happy. She had told Gianna, "Tell Paul I am fine and to please take care of his dad. When the time is right, tell him about your ability. I love them both very much, and I have seen Joey."

She was later buried right alongside Joey. I guess Paul and his dad found some comfort in knowing Joey was truly watching over their precious mom and wife. I also knew Joey was doing a good job helping her upon her arrival in heaven.

After these encounters Paul had with Joey, I recalled something that had happened two months prior to Joey's passing. Paul was on the way to school one morning to pick up his girlfriend at that time. I was also out on the road when I just barely caught a glimpse of his car as he passed by. I came to an intersection fifteen minutes later where I noticed a horrific car accident. From the distance I was at, it appeared to possibly be a fatality. As I drove closer near the scene, I caught sight of Paul! He was slumped over his steering wheel, and he appeared to be in grave condition. His windshield was shattered, and I could only imagine the worst. My thought instantly went to his family, who were still unaware of the accident their only child was involved in. I immediately prayed for intervention. The emergency responders and police were present and waved us forward around the barricade they were now creating. I was upset since I was unable to stop, although I had no choice but to proceed.

Once I pulled over, I called a few others and asked them to extend a prayer of hope for Paul. I knew Joey would be very upset, so I also called home to inform my husband, since Joey was at school and would probably get some news. My husband said he had called home a few minutes ago and was very shaken by the news. I knew we all believed in prayer, and later it was confirmed by Joey that he had done the same. He informed his dad that the school had relayed the message they received from the police and were informed that the accident appeared not to be life threatening. What a relief!

Later that night, the first thing Joey did was to prepare to get down to the hospital where his friend was recovering. As he told me where he was going, I gave him a scapular and sprinkled it with holy water I had saved. Joey later told me, "Mom I placed the scapular around Paul's neck and called him my brother. I also told him to never scare me like that again. I would be devastated if he had not survived." Joey checked in on his friend as often as he was able to hitch a ride from someone who was also visiting him. Thank God Paul recovered, and from that point on, Joey swore to be his body guard since fragments of glass had damaged Paul's ribs. So with this remembered thought, now all that had happened with Joey continuing to call Paul his brother and offer protection on another level, made perfect sense.

Joey had another friend we shared our secret with. He had a few troubles in his life, but he had a good heart. This young man was also on his football team. His name is, Mark. They had also built a great friendship that obviously continues. When Joey was still alive on earth, they had found a way to support each other on and off the football field. Well, the game of life was spelled out within a dream for this friend in ways he would recognize. In a football game! It came at a time in Mark's life when he was searching for guidance and support.

Mark and Joey's friendship initially started as many others, when they were in the middle school. The two of them had a great love for music, and they listened to their collections in our home for hours. They even wrote some of their own songs! The funniest memory I can recall was, when I would pass the room and hear each of them singing! They were young and certainly not afraid of feeling embarrassed by one another. It was a few years later in high school when Mark had to drop out. Joey was very upset, but little could be done at that time to change the situation. Things seemed to deteriorate further for Mark. He found himself removed from school altogether and he was unable to have any further contact.

Mark unfortunately learned about what had happened to Joey while he was away. His family was quick to be at our side to lend help in any way they could. They offered us help through their supportive friendship when our home was filled with people immediately after the tragedy. A few months beyond that, Mark's parents found themselves needing to make a decision within their lives toward a change in direction. He and his family had decided to move out of state. It was some time later, after he and his family were settled within their new home, that he had contacted me. He disclosed to me that he was having dreams of Joey. He said that he very much felt that he needed to describe a particular dream to me. It occurred at a time when he was trying to get his life together and reorganize his goals within hopefully, a straight and narrow path again.

He was very excited to describe how the events unfolded within this in-depth dream. He said he was dressed in his purple and white, football uniform. They were back home on the high school football field. In this dream, it seemed that they were competing in a very important game. The lights, as he recalled, were shining so immensely bright upon the field. Their team was losing very badly at this point in the game and they really needed some reinforcements. The game came to a halt to wait for the needed help to enter the field. There was great anticipation within the players. Of course they and the supporting fans wanted his team to win. Patiently everyone waited to see how the direction of this game could be changed. Suddenly, there were whispers that a very talented and respected player was coming in. The defensive side of the ball would be where the new replacement would hold the needed position.

Mark looked, and all of a sudden, he saw someone approaching wearing the number 34! He rubbed his eyes in confusion as he tried to focus. Next, he noticed that huge, instantly recognizable, contagious smile Joey displayed as he approached closer while walking to his position. Joey then turned and looked back at Mark with his familiar raised eyebrows. He was completely shocked! He knew instantly, without a doubt, that it was him and it all seemed so real. Joey then stepped up to the line as middle linebacker, taking his earthly earned defensive position. Mark all of a sudden became overwhelmed with emotion and rushed to his friend, whom he has missed so much. He could not contain himself and began to cry uncontrollably as he held Joey in a camaraderie bear hug. Joey immediately said in a voice of strength, "Pull yourself together. We're going to win!" Then the game began, and Joey was in his old element, tackling opponents as if they were flies on the field.

When the game had turned the ball over, it was then that Joey had to play his offensive position, fullback. Now they were going to really turn this game around big time in their favor.

Mark counted on Joey's strength and remembered among his teammates and friends, on the field, he was referred to as "the truck." That reference to him was fitting because it was typical to see Joey with opponents hanging on to him as he always pushed forward with all he had. He literally would carry four or five guys on him before he was finally tackled. So the opposing team was completely aware for them to win; Joey would need to be stopped! As the game commenced, Joey began his blocking. Mark now filled the position as the running back and carried the football. (In high school, he was never the running back. However, I think this was just to send Mark a message for all that was going on within his life.) Before he knew it, the ball was in his hands, and he began running down the field to score. That was when he noticed Joey making his very first tackle, and Mark was astonished to see something quite unbelievable: huge white feathers flew out from under his uniform! This dream was really now becoming freaky. Mark was able to contain himself enough because he ran all the way to score a touchdown. (Again as I have said before I'm not taking this dream literally and saying Joey's an angel. I do believe though, it's more of a symbolic message for Mark to know he is by his side and helping him.)

Now Mark suddenly felt he had to help keep these feathers hidden from the fans. Mark did know our secret at this time and must have remembered this in his dream. So next he ran over and quickly tucked them back into his shirt where they wouldn't be seen. The problem now was, Mark was laughing so hard. Once he got past the laughter he shared with Joey, the game was in play again. And as they continued, Joey took another opponent down, and there were those feathers again. Clearly now the momentum had changed within the losing game, and, the more tackles Joey made, the more Mark scored! Before he knew it, the game was over. They had worked very hard together and won!

Then all at once, it seemed that they were now the only ones on the field. Somehow the lights on the field ,were now brighter than ever. Arm in arm, Joey and Mark walked off the field together in victory. Much like how it once was in life.

My take on this whole scenario is, that Joey was sending such a unique and personal extension of love to his friend from heaven. Joey had never forgotten his friend and had sent a message that would really hit home and reinforce the helping hand he was offering still.

Once Mark described the dream to me, I shared my interpretation. I believed that Joey was clearly telling him that if he would play by the rules in life and work hard, he will win. Also, he will help as best he could with the obstacles. The defensive side they played had shown that Joey was at his side while up against many lessons Mark would need to learn. In life, it would be up to Mark who would be learning through his own choices. He would have to carry his burdens just like the ball he carried on the offensive side of the game. Joey will always help where he could to clear the way. If he continued to push ahead in his earthly mission, he would be a winner. Also, I believe many loving spectators were watching from the spirit world, just like the many spectators on the stands during the game. They would be cheering him on along the way, while reminding him to never give up. Then when the game of life is over, Joey will be there waiting for him!

I now knew how important it was to have shared our secret with him. I'm sure Joey knew how healing these dreams were to me as his friends described them. Our secret circle had grown a little, but I knew it was okay.

Soon Joey's first birthday after his passing arrived, and we were sure to celebrate it. I had convinced myself that no matter how painful it was to us, I would never want to exclude him. Ignoring this day or hoping it would fly by unnoticed will not save us from its piercing pain. So instead, we tried to add a thankful element to our reminded memory of his recent passing, to hopefully soften the blow. So on July 13, I made a cake for us all and invited close family members. They all attended; even friends received word of this and were in full support, so many of them joined us. The candles were finally lit, and then we sang, "Happy Birthday." As soon as we finished, Joey immediately appeared to Gianna!

Then Gianna said, "Happy Birthday, Joey."

He replied, "Thank you." Then he immediately vanished. I'm sure he stuck around. Perhaps he knew how difficult this day would be; that's why he chose not to be visible to her. But there were many more visits to come and many more parties for him to attend.

When Gianna's birthday came around a short time later, we were all curious whether Joey would show for the occasion. We, of course, all hoped he would. With this birthday, we were all prepared when the time came to sing, as our eyes were fixed on Gianna. Once we finished, Joey was there. He had not let us down again. Although this time he brought Jessica along, his heavenly helper and now Gianna's friend. All at once, we saw Gianna smiling and she appeared to be greeting people. Next she explained to me, "It had seemed like a parade, Mom." Gianna appeared to be in awe by what she was seeing. She said, "one by one they walked into the room and said, hello!" Soon she greeted even more, as they entered the room acknowledging her. Then she said, "Mom, there are a lot of people here who seem to know me, but I don't know them!"

I was taken a little off guard and considered a thought that may make sense since their attendance seemed harmless, and after all, they were in our presence with Joey, and I knew he would never bring harm to her. Maybe they are people she had known from the other side, before birth. They too seemed to be with us to celebrate and must have wanted her to be aware of their presence. This was another big revelation.

However, from then on, we realized we could always count on visits during future birthdays for the rest of the family members. The occasions within our lives probably are always attended by our spiritual families like weddings, holidays, and births. Then I thought this must occur in all families and unless someone with an ability to see or sense spirit is present, they are not even aware of it.

Before each birthday celebration, I was sure to anticipate his attendance. I always seemed to need to ask a question or two. So Gianna would direct any questions I had to him. And he had plenty of answers she would relay to me. Sometimes I gave her a list, and he never disappointed me because he answered any question he could. Some, however, he said he was unable to answer. I thought, maybe he didn't know the answer or was not allowed to tell us. Maybe because the answers would be coming through his sister and could impact her in some way even though I was *very* careful as to what I would ask. The most important question I needed an answer to was, when he was going to send me a dream visit. This was all I could think of. So many others he knew, had wonderful dreams of him. But I never had one. Why was this happening? After all, I love him so much, I thought to myself. When we asked him, all he said was, "Soon, Mom." I persisted, and he would return with an explanation. It would go like this, "Mom, you think you're ready, but you're not. Believe me; you must be ready for it."

Gee, I thought I was ready. After all, some time has passed now. That must offer strength. I knew I'd become emotional, but I thought certainly I could handle it. I believed to actually see him and to hold him, was really all I needed at this time. I convinced myself I would feel somewhat renewed by this gift of love because it usually, seems so real!

He knew better. He knew what I really needed was further healing within myself, and this would take time. I do know as a bereaved parent, that the wounds run very deep, and everyone is different while handling grief. I thought to myself, *Maybe I am not handling my grief as well as I think I am.* Could I be fooling myself? I pondered on this thought, no, was the answer I immediately thought of. I began to think about the extreme emotions again, that can be the result of a dream visitation. I felt a momentary surge of fear. I then thought, the dream visitation will be wonderful, but then again only a temporary reunion. I couldn't pretend to ignore the hard facts of the situation. Maybe during a dream visit, all I would focus on was how real it seemed. Then I may try to fool myself into believing he had never crossed over.

I assume all of the pieces must be in their rightful place; this must include grief. Timing must be everything. He even went on to tell Gianna, "Everyone has a door within them, and this door needs to be open. You need to welcome me into your heart." I have read how grief can also be a barrier to those in spirit. I guess maybe it is really a form of self-protection to remain in place until I can handle all the buried-deep emotions that also come along within a visit. This was also something I needed to work on.

More friends and family who have had visitation dreams later reconfirmed to me that it indeed, resurfaced their initial phase of grief. When they had woken up, they became flooded with despair towards facing the loss again, which they had been trying to recover from. So when I prayed and pleaded for a dream, it soon became clear he had heard me. Although it seemed that the dream I so longed for had to be delivered to me indirectly at this point in time, somehow different than my expectation. A gentler way perhaps was all I could handle, so instead, he did the next best thing: Joey sent another dream to a close friend of his. This friend was a girl who had attended school in town. She also was in Joey's senior class, and in fact, they had been friends throughout the years since childhood. Her name is Karen.

One night, as Karen slept, she had an amazing and very vivid dream. She drifted off to sleep and soon she became a little startled. In the distance, there was Joey; he was dressed in a black tuxedo. (We had buried him in this attire, and she had no idea since we chose not to have a wake service.) She soon realized she was within a familiar place. They were back at the high school they had both attended. Karen also noticed, that she together with their familiar friends, were within the school cafeteria. Then Joey entered the room. As soon as they noticed, they all rushed to him immediately. They all hugged him and continually asked him where he had been all this time. He said he's been gone for a little while, but now he's back.

They were all so happy as they surrounded him. Then she looked to the corner of the room and saw me. I stood there crying, and quickly Joey walked up to me and hugged me. She said it was then that she woke up, thinking for a moment how real it all was.

After a few minutes, a sudden rush of grief overwhelmed her. She then realized it was all just a dream, and her friend was in heaven. But somehow the way it played out had her believing there was more to it. Karen knew she had to come to my house and tell me immediately, even though she had a prior engagement that afternoon. Once she arrived at my house, she immediately described the whole dream to me. I instantly felt he had sent this dream for us both. I assured her it was a good thing and that I had prayed and pleaded for a dream desperately, unafraid of whatever consequences may occur.

When she told me what he was wearing, I said, "Yes, we did bury him in his tuxedo!" She was so shocked and also believed me as I told her all I had learned about dream visits and how I really believed in them. So in a roundabout way, I received what I needed, but not exactly how I had wanted it.

All of these dreams really helped to secure a foundation toward real strength. Yet we still did have so much more to face. The next hurdle would be the upcoming football season. Many of Joey's old teammates were now in their senior year of high school. This year, they dedicated their season to honor their fallen friend. It had now become so difficult to drive by that field and not become upset. We had so many happy memories prior to this tragedy.

A few weeks into the season, we were invited for a game in which some of Joey's old teammates would be playing. I was scared to death in attending any games, and I know my husband was also, even though he didn't admit it. The pain would be so acute and I was afraid of facing it. The school had now decided to retire Joey's football number 34. No one in the future on the high school football team will ever wear this number. We felt very honored and knew we must attend.

As the players entered the field, they ran and gave a slap to the scoreboard in support of Joey. He had done this so many times in the past just prior to a game. Next, they all mimicked Joey's Tarzan yell at the conclusion of the National Anthem. They even took time out to touch the stone; the school had painted it purple in his honor shortly after his passing. (A few weeks later, my husband had added a spray painted 34 and also the name Stone upon it.) As it was time to begin the game, I felt the emotion that swiftly filled the field. I would like to think that they had expected heavenly help from their buddy.

There was a small ceremony to begin in this tribute to Joey. The principal marched onto the field carrying a glass frame enclosing Joey's North Branford jersey within it. A wave of grief began at my toes and spread throughout my entire body! How painful that was. Next we were honored as we were given the team ball during the halftime break. This would become a treasure to us as an example of Joey's teammates' love for him.

For that football season, each game always ended to add up to a combined score of 34. How that was accomplished, I may never know. Joey's jersey still hangs there today, over a decade later, outside of the school's gymnasium.

CHAPTER 8

VALIDATION

You try convincing yourself to believe something
Yet somewhere, someway, it rings a bell of truth
As a piece of information is delivered
It could mean the world to you
The words may be foreign to others
But from deep inside you, it ignites a spark
Following it are waves of faith and hope
That helps you rebuild, so you can go on.

I have found out how important validation is to us. It is considerably strengthening. I have been very lucky to receive such a considerable amount. It has reinforced my faith and hope, for I now know my son and the other deceased family members are fine and are watching over us. They will all be there when I, my husband, and other family members cross over.

Validation did come to me many times in all of the many visits Gianna had, including all the dream visits that continued to come to so many people connected to Joey. However, validation did come in other ways.

One night, Joe, Joey's father, felt as if Joey was hugging him. He began to fall off to sleep not long after his passing and felt his presence and warmth that surrounded and consumed him. He said it was wonderful.

On one of Joey's visits to Gianna, we asked him about this occurrence.

"He felt that? It was a *love hug*," Joey announced to Gianna. It obviously was delivered by Joey to his dad. While all this is comforting, I can't stop from having my many questions. I am continually haunted over and over as I daily face this tragic loss of my son. Is there any way all this could have been avoided? This question still continues to consume me; it's hard to truly get it in my head.

Another question that remained to reside within me is, how this could have happened to our family. Could this truly have been Joey's destiny? Then I recall a dream my husband, Joe, had before Joey's passing. Joe's mom and dad were divorced when he was very young. He had lived with his mom, sister, and grandparents. He looked upon his grandparents as a second pair of parents and loved them deeply, so when they passed away, he was shattered.

One night, in the year 2000, two years before Joey's passing, my husband drifted off to sleep next to me in bed. I heard him emitting some strange sounds, and I wasn't sure if he was really sleeping. My husband is a real jokester, so naturally I thought he was up to his old tricks. So at first I chuckled; then I noticed something else was going on. He was dreaming and clearly very upset. I stopped what I had been reading and turned to him, and he suddenly woke up after a minute or two. He was very much shaken and would not tell me what happened at first. When I pressed him for answers, he went on to tell me how he had dreamt of his grandfather. He said he found himself in front of the home he had lived in with his grandparents, when he was much younger. He said that he approached the door and then entered into the kitchen, which was very dark. He began searching for the light switch when he suddenly felt his grandfather's presence very strongly. He said he couldn't see him, although somehow he knew he was there. He couldn't figure out how he knew this. Then he had an overwhelming intense feeling of love emanating from his grandfather to him. He said his grandfather then wanted to kiss him on the cheek as he did so many times before, throughout his childhood. He became very fearful at this point. As his grandfather's presence grew closer to him, he became very upset. (I thought at the time, maybe this was because he had missed and loved him so much that it had caused him to freak out within the dream.) When his dream seemed to be almost too much to handle, he snapped out of it and woke up.

I believe this was a type of prophetic dream due to Joe's grandfather in spirit knowing that Joe would be losing his only son, Joey from earth. It made no sense of course at the time, but now after the loss, it does. In some way I believe he was attempting to prepare him. Possibly this was a message that only his soul would understand and Joe knowing his grandfather had great love for them both, that he would be offering his help as best as he could. Another possibility to add to all of this, was that he would realize his grandfather, was truly alive on the other side. And that would help validate Joe's belief in life after death, when he would be needing it, after Joey's crossing over. This was without a doubt a great gift of love. I always think back to this because upon our first visit with Marti, the medium healer, she turned to my husband and said, "Your grandfathers have had your back for some time." (Joe had also lost a grandfather on his dad's side when he was very young.) She went on to say how they were trying to help him with the overwhelming pain and not to worry about the boy, for they, among others, had him with them. He was fine and very much loved.

Joe's Grandfathers continued by revealing to Marti that they had seen what was coming. I believe what they were saying was that Joey's crossing over to heaven could not have been changed. It was somehow part of God's plan. As I think about this my belief is further reinforced that no one is ever lost to us, and they still see us and are truly helping us from heaven. This new revelation along with other experiences of my own had also contributed towards building my strength.

When I was young, I had an occurrence that began to open my mind wide toward realizing spiritual possibilities. I was only twelve years old at the time when I went to visit extended family in Italy with my great-grandmother. It was an exciting vacation for me, full of unknown opportunity. Nonie, my great-grandmother, was fully capable of meeting the demands of vacationing with a twelve-year-old girl. We were to stay with an uncle in the outskirts of Rome. We would be there for five long weeks. Upon our many excursions, visiting one most important destination was to stop at the Vatican and get a glimpse of the pope. We attended a mass and I was mesmerized by his presence when that opportunity arrived. Back home, I had attended Catholic school and held my religious upbringing in the highest regard. Prayer was always a morning and nightly routine for me. It was unusual not to find me with a pair of rosary beads around my neck. Often at night, I had laid in bed after a prayer, enjoying the silence. Little did I know, this was a form of meditation for me. But I was a child and knew only that it had always helped me to feel better.

After a short time in Italy, I had become extremely homesick, to put it mildly. I had met my many unknown aunts, uncles, and cousins. They all seemed so kind, but nothing could replace the home I had left behind in America. I truly missed the faces of my mom, dad, brother, and sisters. I felt like I had fallen from the sky and landed on another planet. I begged God to send me home, somehow. About two weeks into the trip, I became very physically sick. I believe I had the flu. Whatever the illness was, it definitely was compounded along with my homesickness. One evening, after Nonie and I turned in for the night, something amazing happened. I was feeling especially under the weather earlier that particular evening. Around four or five in the morning, I woke up feeling very cold. So I stood up between the side-by-side beds and walked over to retrieve a blanket, which was on a small table, located across from the footboards of the two beds. As I began to walk, I looked to my left and noticed the large doors that led to an outside patio were not completely closed. So I tiptoed over and closed them tightly to remove the chill I was feeling. I then picked up the blanket and carried it with me back to bed. A strange feeling came over me as the thoughts of loneliness streamed through my head. I wished I was home again. I remembered it was unrealistic, and this made me very sad.

All at once I noticed, as I looked down to the end of our beds, a brilliant and overwhelming light appeared. It was emanating from a large white figure that was floating. I believe it was a female because this figure was wearing a beautiful, full flowing white gown. However, as I briefly looked I noticed she didn't have any feet! That was all it took, and I completely freaked out! She was clearly at least two feet off the ground.

At that moment I recalled each and every scary movie I had seen and loved to watch so much. You can imagine the thoughts a twelve-year-old had running through her mind. Without taking another look at the apparition, under the blankets I went. All I could do was scream as loud as possible to get my Nonie's attention. I needed her protection so desperately at that very moment. I can still remember how my heart pounded as my fear grew.

"Nonie! Nonie! Nonie!" I screamed.

Nonie had always slept beside me each night. However, she was in a deep sleep and she didn't immediately hear me. But by now, I was so overwhelmed with sweat and fear, I almost couldn't breath. Just then I heard her say, "what?, what's the matter?" I then had to find the courage to emerge from under the blankets. Finally, after Nonie's continual reassurance, I felt safe enough to open my eyes. I then blurted out all that had happened. As Nonie listened to me with all her attention, I glanced throughout the room. Then I noticed the most unsettling part of all. The patio doors clearly were no longer locked closed. They were wide open! Now I really didn't know what to make of this.

Next, the room quickly filled with my aunts and uncle who had been sleeping, but now were all wide-awake. As I told my story, they tried to convince me of all kinds of explanations. The curtains, my imagination, etc.

Nothing could sway my thinking. I knew what I had seen. It was very real. This was a huge step to confirm my belief in heaven. As I grew older, I remembered this occurrence often. I concluded with the thought that it must have been a guide or an angel coming to offer me healing and reassurance. Possibly, believing this initiated the validation that needed to grow much later in life? I now know that there is no doubt in the spirit world, because I definitely saw it with my own eyes.

As life continues, I hold onto my past revelations and keep my eyes open for the signs of the future. They seemed to be a constant and ongoing gift of love. I continue to discover them and will remain open for all I can receive. My Joey's football number on his high school team was 34; it seemed that I was continually seeing it everywhere. The second Father's Day since Joey's passing had especially caught our attention. The three-digit lottery number for that night was 034. I guess after one occurrence you may think, "Well, that's a coincidence." However, it must be honored just the same because it was quickly becoming a huge calling card of Joey's. I took it as a gift from him to his father as if saying, "Happy Father's Day, Dad."

I revealed my thoughts to my husband, and deep inside, I knew he wanted to believe. He was somewhat surprised, but clearly needed more convincing. So each time I experienced something, I brought it to his attention. Soon, even Joey's friends were telling us upon a visit, how the number 34 had been showing up a lot for them at weird times. A few commented on when they would travel and how they were led to room 34 or seat 34. They were surprised because clearly they had done nothing to provoke this happening, but I was dropping hints often, as possibly being a sign from Joey. I soon would have a huge 34 sign of my own.

I had found peace with all of Gianna's and Marti's many messages, but I also found comfort in reading books for further understanding of the many spiritual dynamics. After all, my son was there, so I had an unending craving to educate myself completely for further salvation of his welfare. So I was always in search of a good book on the subject. As I read through each book I purchased, it wasn't long before I was searching for another. There were a few I didn't find all that helpful in what comfort I had desired. Then when I came across a favorite, I purchased more copies to offer anyone else I might meet experiencing grief.

One day in July (Joey's birthday month), I was shopping in Barnes and Noble. It had been over a year since my son's passing, but clearly I was still a very brokenhearted mom, and this month was an especially tough one. I approached the register after selecting my many copies of a particular book to offer others. I then dropped them on the counter and waited for the total. The cashier said, "That will be $34.34 please." Well, I was taken completely off guard and shocked. I stood there for a moment in disbelief and began to shake all over. I now knew this was clearly a sign, and there was no dismissing it. The only way to describe it is to say that it felt like a love shot directed right to my wounded heart. My hope was lifted, and I flashed the kind of smile upon my face that had been gone for a long, long time. My Joey clearly realized I was having a rough day and knew I would recognize his sign. Nothing can replace the reinforcing exhilaration that consumed me.

His father also had experienced this same sign a few weeks later. He was at a store making a purchase, and the same thing happened. "That will be $34.34," the cashier said. I think he then pinched himself, because he had heard me tell the family of my experience with the number 34. I had realized at the time, he was only an earshot away and clearly did it purposely. I was elated as I had hoped this would strengthen his belief. I guess Joey had a hand in boosting his belief also. As time went on, it seemed he continued to be inundated with many signs. His next sign occurred when he went golfing. He was so shocked since no matter when he arrived, he almost always ended up with golf cart number 34.

Another day I stopped at the store to make a purchase. The cashier handed me my change. I looked at one of the dollar bills, and there was a 34 written at the top of it! I thought to myself, *Am I really seeing this?*

Well, Joey was only beginning with his many 34 signs. Some weeks later, I was on the highway, and of course, thoughts of Joey were always on my mind. I was heading to a religious store to find something there to offer me more comfort. All of a sudden, I noticed a gold corvette pulling very quickly toward my car. It had drawn my attention because I thought it might hit me. As I took a quick look, something caught my eye.

As I focused my eyes, I was shocked by what I was seeing. The car had a license plate number 34! I mean only a 34, not another letter or number. It had pulled directly in front of me and continued down the highway until we came to an exit, a few miles further, where it drove off. It sent shivers through me, and again I knew it was another sign. Boy I thought to myself, that Joey sure was working hard, and I love it!

Another sign I recall after Joey's passing, was when my employer notified me of an accident insurance policy I had on myself and my family. I had completely forgotten about it because I initially took it out to protect me from any injuries that would cause me to lose income.

So when the claim papers were delivered, I just couldn't fill them out. Instead I asked my sister, who had helped us fill out other documents that my husband and I had great difficulty with. She was willing to help again, and I will forever be grateful for such a loving and selfless act.

Once it was completed and I signed it, in the mail it went. I had put it out of my mind until one day there was a knock on the door. When I opened it, there was a female UPS driver holding an envelope. I then noticed the insurance name on it and knew it was the check. She handed me a clip board. As I reached to grasp the board, she announced, "Mrs. Stone, please sign on line 34." I was so shocked because I expected an unhappy dose of intense grief upon the delivery. I didn't want to be reminded of that horrible day. Clearly a sign hadn't even crossed my mind. I was taken completely off guard. But when I saw the 34, my thoughts changed. It had softened the blow and lifted my spirits. It changed my thoughts to receiving love from him. It seems that my son has a unique way of continually helping me. Signs seemed to develop out of the blue when I wasn't even looking for them.

Then I believe he realized the need was growing in gaining his father's attention, so he also continued to get more of his own signs. Once, my husband was looking through his monthly skiing magazine. When he glanced through the magazine he turned to a page filled with only football players. He looked in disbelief as every player wore a shirt displaying a huge 34! One even had a huge number 34 painted on his face. I still think my husband remained a little bit on the fence with entirely believing as much as I now did. Maybe it was more of a way of preparing himself to be able to cope with the fear he held within himself, if in fact, life after death really wasn't possible. However, the many signs always put a smile on his face just the same. I knew it was clear; Joey was continually doing his best to extend heavenly assurance, any way he could.

Other signs were Joey's favorite songs that seemed to play at appropriate times. Often at times or in places you wouldn't expect it. The one song that was newly released had me really thinking of him. From the first time I listened to it, it had me in tears. I often would hear it as I entered a store or just turned on my car radio. It was Train's "Calling All Angels." As I listened to the words, I associated my own meaning to my son. I had always felt so protected by Joey when he was physically here. I still feel protected by unseen guidance. The song helps me recognize those feelings, and I really feel a bond of strength as I listen to it. The song even made some reference to football and had a line that plays over and over in my head.

"I won't give up, if you don't give up."

Marti had told us Joey's protection was still given to his family and friends from where he was now, as he did so often on earth while in the physical body. So it is no surprise in this next experience that his loving protection was extended to his father. This occurrence was a turning point to convince him of everything I was becoming increasingly more and more convinced of. One rainy day, my husband was returning from an out-of-town business trip. He was driving on the highway in the fast lane. His phone rang; just as he went to grab the phone, he noticed another car driven by a teenager swerving over into his lane. He was traveling extremely fast and he hadn't even noticed Joe. Upon noticing the sense of danger, Joe immediately dropped the phone. He then quickly swerved his car over to avoid being hit. This led him down an embankment, now traveling at a speed clearly not for maintaining any sense of control in this situation. Worst of all, he was in a vehicle that has been recently known to be quite prone to roll over in some situations. Joe was not panicking but fully expected the rollover at any time. Both of his hands remained tightly gripped upon the steering wheel, and he knew he should not apply the brakes at all.

Then once the vehicle slowed down and he again had total control of it, he began to return up the embankment to resume driving. He had noticed other drivers had stopped to watch, obviously fully expecting to witness a terrible accident. As he finally reached the highway, immediately a song began to play on the car radio. It was "Calling All Angels."

I don't know exactly how this was achieved at that precisely needed moment, although I do think my husband now believed Joey had a hand in protecting him. Joe was clearly overwhelmed as he relayed the story to me later.

As time went on, we were still given further proof of how Joey continued to watch over us. My young daughter Gabrielle had fallen onto an end table at home. She had cut her head and was bleeding badly. At that time, I was at the store, and my husband called me on my cell phone and said I needed to meet him at the hospital. It quickly became evident to me, that he was very upset, as he rambled the details of all that had occurred. I rushed out of the store to my car, and of course I was continually praying and asking for Joey's help. I kept reassuring myself he would be aware of the situation. Then as I drove off, two young teenagers caught my attention as they walked past my car. I looked, and one of them was wearing a shirt, which of course, had a huge 34 on it! There was my sign; I thought he must be sending me confirmation of his help.

Soon I arrived at the hospital and met my husband, Gianna, and Gabrielle. Gabrielle seemed very frightened and she was crying. I held her in my arms and sat down to wait for a doctor. After which seemed to be quite a long while, she and I, along with Gianna, were led into a cubical by a nurse. My husband and I agreed that he needed to go home and tend to the other children, since it seemed things would now be under control. He knew Gabrielle needed her mom.

In the past, Gabrielle was so often comforted and protected by her brother Joey. I was worried because I knew she probably needed a shot for pain and then stitches. She was very afraid of needles. My thoughts went to Joey, as I recall when he was young and needed stitches. I luckily had my sister with me at that time. She had stood next to him as the nurses held him tightly to perform the procedure. I couldn't handle looking, but now I knew I had to be strong and face that fear again. I was thinking of how much I wished Joey was here to help her through this as an older brother. As I continued to soothe her, my thoughts turned into a prayer while I focused on my daughter.

We had been waiting now for such a long time, as I wondered when a doctor would finally come in to tend to her. A few moments later, Gianna announced that Joey was there. She started to laugh loudly as she described Joey beginning to act as his very familiar and humorous self. She said he stuck only his head out from around the outside of the curtained room we were in. Then his huge eyes, which had always seemed to sparkle, were now focused on us with warmth. He then—as he always did in life—lifted his eyebrows as he was trying to lighten the serious situation. Joey then stepped forward a little. Quickly Gianna noticed he was dressed in a green gown, the same as the doctors here in the hospital wore. He really went all out on calming his sister's fears as we listened to Gianna's description of all that was happening. He even had on a surgical mask, and Gianna said it looked like he was wearing a new pair of brown shoes for the occasion. She continued to say it looked similar to a pair of shoes their father had. He pulled down his mask and lovingly said, "Hi." He then told Gianna to tell Gabrielle that she will be all right and that the whole ordeal would pinch a little and last for only a few seconds. He also reminded Gianna of how he watches over all of us. He gave us his love and then said good-bye.

This seemed to do the trick, because Gabrielle seemed to be more at ease. Everything after that happened just as he had said it would, and I was fully capable of helping her through it. The protection and love he sent us remains very clear and reassuring.

Even with all the validation we are so lucky to have, it still continues to be a very difficult road. Nothing removes the pain we all still must face. For me, I found that my nights seemed to be the hardest when the quiet would run emotions of the day over and over within my mind. All thoughts seemed to be filled with the reminders of my loss. They seemed to be an inescapable and constant haunt.

I knew I somehow needed to find a little diversion out of the house for a while. Fortunately, I believe we found a break from the wave of pain that still ran deeply throughout our home. Gianna and a few of the other family members would jump in the car with me and go for a ride together, usually in the evening. We would play Joey's music and think of him while I would drive. It seemed to help sooth our pain and also allowed us to feel close to him. Joey was always a huge music lover in life. Soon we discovered how he used this as an opportunity for an additional means of communication.

As we listened to music in the car and all of our thoughts were of him, he would surprise us and appear to Gianna! She would see him standing there alongside the road as we drove by, beaming with a familiar ear to ear grin. This new discovery was very helpful to lighten our wounded hearts. Gianna would hold our every bit of attention as she described the scene. She said that he was always surrounded in an immense light. We all flooded her with questions to ask him, and she delivered them. Joey then gave her answers filled with love and hope.

Something he has repeated more than once during these rides were, "I am alive!" It has been often said, that we are more alive once home in heaven than we ever were here.

We were becoming very entertained as he included his sense of humor during these visits. It was becoming more and more clear to us that Joey was very happy. Sometimes he would even show up in a Superman costume to really crack us up. I'm sure he knew how we would react, since his friends called him Superman when he was in high school. Other times we listened to songs that frequently had been played during a practice, prior to his high school football games. Then as these were played, Joey would show up in his football outfit. This was all too much to believe! But every bit of it is true! He lifted our spirits like only he could do.

He put forward all his best efforts within his unique personality. We found ourselves longing for our rides. Sometimes, it was not only him who would show up. He would bring others. A few times, relatives who had passed away appeared, and other times it was friends we had known. Then still other times, spirits who we didn't know would show up. These rides became an almost-sure way of Joey connecting to us. Many times before we were out of the driveway prior to turning the music on, he was already there. I guess this was another way of him letting us know, he is watching over us.

One night, we were on our way somewhere and had not put on any music yet. Gianna turned around and was startled because he was sitting right behind her seat in the car! All he said was, "Hi!"

Gianna replied, "Oh my God, you scared me, Joey!"

That was the last time he did that.

All of these happenings were so healing and helpful for us. But, we still needed to keep this to ourselves since we were sure anyone other than Marti and our trusted friends and family, would think we were nuts! During all of these occurrences, we were so grateful and felt so lucky, but I still always wanted more. So as soon as I woke up in the morning, I immediately tried to focus my attention upon all of the signs coming from Joey, each day.

As a family, we were becoming more and more aware of the many possibilities for spiritual contact. Soon, our awareness became even further broadened with still another occurrence. One day in December, my husband turned on the computer to check his e-mail. As he looked down the list, one message immediately caught his attention. He clicked on it to read it entirely. To his surprise, the message appeared like this: "Is This What You Wanted?" (Then a lot of numbers after it.) Followed by; "JoJo Loves Ya Lots." This was the nickname we gave Joey when he was a little boy. The e-mail went on to promote generic prescriptions. He then called me into the room. Soon, some of the girls followed, and they were just as excited. We all scratched our heads in amazement. After a while, I think they brushed it off a little as coincidence. However, I knew it was no coincidence and was in fact a little step closer toward helping him to believe. I just accepted it as another validation that came our way.

Yet there are still more validating stories to tell. Such as when others we knew were searching for comfort within their own struggles. An immediate family member had a friend, who had faced the passing of a loved one. She had been seeking communication with the help of another local and well-known medium.

As the reading began, her loved one came through with many validating and healing messages. She was so excited and hung onto every loving word delivered to her. The messages were many, then all of a sudden, this medium began to ask if she knew a Joey. She further delivered the fact that he had drowned. Then she said he was holding a 3 and a 4.

"What does the number 34 mean to you?" she asked. "Who is Marianne that has four girls?" Now she was completely bewildered since she was not recognizing the information the medium was giving her. She was hoping to hear from a friend that had crossed over so that's where her focus was. Then the medium said he is on a very high level, much like the level of an angel. With that, she finished by saying that he is swinging a golf club. (My husband had started an annual golf tournament. It honored Joey and continued to deliver his message, while in support of high school students.)

After the session was over and she was returning home, she pondered over the information she had received. Then all of a sudden, it dawned on her. The medium was talking about Joey, her friend (my husband) Joe's son. Quickly, it all seemed to make sense to her. She began thinking about when she had learned of Joey's passing and had felt so bad for her friend Joe. She realized, it was a chance for her to deliver the information she had received. She phoned our home and was so excited to inform Joe of the message. It proves spirit will also use you to deliver a message for others at times. It appeared that somehow with her telling her friend, it took on a greater meaning of validation, and I believe it helped them both.

CHAPTER 9

THE MIRACLE OF GIANNA

Love is never lost
Hope sees us through
Faith restores

Gianna always amazed us with her insight. Her purity and innocence always captured my attention and continues still today. I
always knew she had an independence about her. And she always
seemed to be quite content with all the love that was directed her
way! And now she was growing into a strong and loving person who
has an open connection to the spirit world. Her ability had begun
to be broadened. She continued to have other visits that occurred
completely out of the blue.

For example, we had noticed one day, that our dog Lucky
appeared to be focusing his attention towards the ceiling while
barking at no one. At first, we really didn't pay it much attention
since we were still dealing with so much. However, he persisted and
eventually drew our attention. We couldn't understand it initially;
it seemed totally out of sorts for him. He certainly was not a stu-
pid dog. Over the short time we had owned him, he was quickly
housebroken. And Gianna had taught him many tricks, which he
performed at her request. He only barked when someone entered
the house and then again when they left. So it made no sense to us,
as he continued to bark at the thin air.

One night in particular, I stopped as I was walking by Lucky and he began to bark at the air again. When Gianna entered the room, she quickly announced that we had another visitor. I said a quick prayer and stood by this visitor in silence as she received information. Gianna went on to identify her as one of my son's female acquaintances. My daughter said did she not know this girl or how she had made her transition to the other side. (Later I did recall this visitor and realized she did have struggles within her life, and Joey had brought warmth and comfort to her by his kindness.)

The next day in the kitchen, I was scanning the newspaper, and soon realized I was in the obituary section when suddenly I noticed her picture. I called Gianna into the room but I didn't tell her anything.

As if she anticipated what I was thinking she simply walked in and pointed to the picture and said, "That's her." And then she walked out of the room.

I was stunned that she was able to identify her so quickly. I assume Gianna had been recognized by the spirit world with her ability. I admit though at times I still became a little shaken by it.

Gianna had a few of these unannounced visitors. This next encounter really left me in amazement. As you know, we took rides a lot to get a change of scenery while connecting with Joey in a humorous and entertaining way. One night, as we were out, Gianna yelled to me, "Mom, stop you're going to hit someone from heaven!" As you could have guessed, I was shocked and didn't know what to make of this bizarre statement. Then she explained to me that she saw a well-dressed man holding a few specific items, which seemed to complete his ensemble. He had a newspaper clutched under his arm as well as an umbrella. He also had the same lines filled with white bright light emanating from within him. However, his lines of light were not extended as far as others. I didn't know what to make of it, so we just chalked it off as something we couldn't explain.

Soon he seemed to be showing up more and more. Gianna even saw him in our yard; he was asking her to help him. *Help him with what?* I thought.

On one of Joey's visits, she asked him what it was all about and what he wanted from her. All he said was, "Help him." Almost as if she somehow already had known how to help this man.

Quite often, she noticed him when we were out on our nightly rides, but always just as we drove over a hill. Each time he was dressed the same and seemed to be walking across the street. Then I remembered from my younger years before I was married, an incident where a man was instantly killed while walking. Prior to this tragedy, occasionally my family would give him rides and over time became friendly with him. I thought more about it and recalled that the way this man was dressed now, was the same as he had dressed many years ago; then it all began to fit. I again was surprised as I tried to make sense of it all, but at least now I knew who this was.

His appearance continued to occur over the course of many months, but one day another strange incident happened. My husband was in our bedroom, and the television was on. Then all at once it turned off, all by itself. He called to me, while announcing this, because he was really unsure of what just occurred. We knew he still had a hard time believing *everything*, so I admit we kept him a little out of the loop. I said to him as I entered the room very nonchalantly, "You must have touched the remote control." I tried to first offer a logical explanation and was hoping that's all it was.

He quickly replied, "The remote is over there on the other side of the room!"

I thought, *Oh my God, can someone be here?*

So I called for my daughter quickly. "Gianna, come here please."

As soon as she entered the room, I realized she was speaking to someone. I quickly asked her, and she told me it was this same spirit who we have been seeing crossing the road.

He then asked her again to help him. She responded by asking him to meet her outside. I didn't know what the heck to make of this latest encounter, but I knew she must have an idea. So I remained close enough by her while also believing she would be protected.

So I watched her go down the back stairs of the deck, then walk over to the garage area. I went outside to tend to my garden that was very close by while still keeping an eye on her. It quickly seemed as if she was speaking to someone. After a short time she returned inside and appeared to be very happy. I then asked her for all the details. Gianna said she began to pray, and very soon after that, an unbelievable vision began to unfold. A great angel seemed to float down and wrap an arm around the man that was now before her. They then floated up and seemed to enter into something and all of a sudden disappear. She knew she had helped him. The exact way the man was helped is unclear but somehow she believed he would find the happiness he had sought. When Joey had visited again, he told her that indeed she had helped him.

She never heard or saw him again. I recall reading how some people aren't always aware that they have crossed over, when it is sudden. However, you still are you. Maybe he was afraid and needed the aide of an angel. All I could think about, was why was it that Gianna was the one to help him. I guess somehow she just knew how. Possibly his attention was only fixed upon the living, and this created his ability to become lost. Trusting the innocence of a child may have been easier for him. We were very happy he had found his way back home.

CHAPTER 10

A QUEST FOR TRUTH

Take with you what you need
Leave the rest behind
A vow to learn all you can
Your soul recognizes a truth
Which is meant for you, upon your path

"No blame," "no shame," and "no guilt" are words I cannot forget. These words filled my head in one of my earliest readings with Marti. I guess blame is one feeling I felt I had needed. As I look within, I ask myself, "How can I be here? There must be someone or something that is at fault." This thought seems to alleviate the phrase that plays over and over in my mind: "I should've," "I could've," and "I would've."

Although in Joey's case, there truly was no blame. I cannot speak for others in different circumstances. However, I can say that if you let it, it will consume you piece by piece. Try to let go and give it to God. I believe when justice is warranted, it will be served either in your time or God's. No one will escape consequence when a person has knowingly inflicted harm to another. It simply is against God's law, which above all is love.

When I first had a reading with Marti, Joey's message was that it was his time. Nothing could have been changed. Joey also affirmed this to Gianna. Maybe it is all a part of God's plan. I can't understand it now, but I will try and search for the truth. Truth, I felt, was another ingredient towards survival.

Now shame is something I recognized. Why, I don't know. Joey, or I, didn't do anything wrong. Yet the stigma of an untimely loss created feelings of shame, a feeling that seemed to overshadow me because of the most unimaginable tragedy that occurred. I found myself ducking from people when I ventured out. I didn't want to be confronted. I thought, *what is going through their minds?* Now when I remember this, I understand, that it really is foolish. How would Joey feel with this undeserving thought? I began to face these feelings with memories of Joey and how proud I am of him. Shame is clearly unfounded and would stand for a weakening of the soul. I asked myself, *how can I continue to help spread his message with feelings of shame at the same time?* My love for Joey won. I overcame this feeling with my new determined strength. This is another feeling I chose to leave behind.

No guilt. Wow, now this is entirely a whole different feeling. The thought of not being able to protect when I really needed to, appeared to be mostly where it was coming from. Early after our loss, people were with us constantly. After a short time, they needed to return to their own lives again. This is understandable; everyone has his or her own obligations. This distance was hard because it only strengthened the unsettled feelings I now must face. Guilt was definitely one of them. I believe this is a common feeling when living with a loss and faced with your own survival.

Compassion from friends and family is what I needed most, and that feeling was shared and offered by many of them.

I now had to allow Joey to fulfill the role intended for him. So instead of harboring these unhealthy feelings, I would courageously face them and realize they didn't belong to me. I would embrace the love that I chose to recognize as being extended to me from Joey. I then would reveal all that I had learned so people who needed it, would receive it, and hopefully it would help them.

I will continue to search and find a way to hear my son's entire message. I will deliver it as best as I can. I think of my son as a great teacher, a teacher that is our equal but is filled with a deeper level of accumulated knowledge his soul brought into the world. He always demonstrated unconditional love among his peers and family, with an undeniable ability to spread this awareness.

This was further delivered through Joey's connections and actions to help all. He has taught me far more than I had ever taught him. This knowledge is similar to a torch. Once lit, it can become ever so bright, and as we turn to touch another's torch, it ignites and then becomes infectious. This light could then continue to forever spread and grow. We all are on a path of love and understanding with an ability to unite and become one.

CHAPTER 11

A LEGEND IN THE MAKING

Our actions create how we are remembered
It manifests love in many unforeseen ways
While it's rippling effect has the power to grow.

Much of the help Joey offered to people were not always apparent to my husband or myself. His actions were always for the benefit of helping others. It was almost as if he was preprogrammed and was continually operating in an autopilot mode. We became more informed of a few incidents after his passing, but many we just simply were not aware of. These stories continue to instill the pride and realization of all he stood for and continues still today.

Just before Joey's sophomore year of high school ended, there was a graduation party at a senior student's house. Joey had made many friends that would be graduating, so he was invited. Once at the party, all seemed to be going well and really uneventful. As the evening progressed, Joey needed to use the facilities, so he went looking upstairs since the bottom floor was already occupied. He began walking through the hallway and suddenly stopped in his tracks when he thought he had heard a friend's muffled screams. He then listened for a moment, and he soon realized that he had recognized the female voice. He then heard a voice of the male gender that obviously was ignoring her pleas or reasoning. He followed his instincts and stepped towards a closed door. He called out to her and heard this friend frantically call out his name in response to him.

Immediately Joey burst into the room and his concerns were confirmed as he saw his friend being wrestled to the ground by this guy. Joey jumped right into action as he rushed over and grabbed him, since he needed strong convincing to leave. There was no question she was very grateful for Joey defending her. When Joey relayed brief details of the occurrence to my husband a few days later, we clearly didn't receive every detail of his further protection. He never needed to boast about himself. He just simply did what was right.

I was given greater detail in the year of 2002, a few short months after Joey's passing away. It was on his birthday. This was among the few times in which I bravely visited his grave, but I am so glad that I did. There I found a note in full description of all that had happened that night, so very long ago. The note was just lying there and was not in a sealed envelope, so I felt it would be okay to read it. Much of the details that occurred that night were described in it and I was already familiar with. That was until she said how her father had been told recently all that had transpired and was deeply moved. Also, how he wasn't given the chance to thank Joey. She went further to say how much she loved and appreciated his actions in her time of need. She also mentioned how Joey's actions continued to offer her protection that evening, even when it was clear that she was safe. He didn't leave her sight since she was still so shaken up by the whole ordeal. So he found a blanket and slept on the floor by the bed where she slept. All night he remained there so he was sure she would be safe. He told her that someone would have to get by him before they got to her! What a wonderful gift that was to receive. Of course, it immediately brought tears to my eyes and made me cherish him even more!

Still, there were many other stories we also became aware of after the tragedy. However, the following is among my favorites. A few weeks after Joey's passing, a friend of his, whom we didn't recognize initially, was standing outside our front door. We happily allowed him to come in as it appeared he was there to comfort us, as well as to seek comfort for himself. He introduced himself as Larry. After the ice was initially broken and we spoke for a while about how our lives were changed, he began to deliver a story about Joey's heroism at a much earlier age. This incident, as he explained, happened when he and Joey were in the middle school. Joey was approximately around twelve years of age. Larry may have been a year younger. They were at a party with friends which was held at another's house. While many people were inside, Larry and a few others remained socializing outside. These few guests, for whatever reason, soon began to taunt Larry and then bully him. Quickly he became consumed with fear since he was clearly outnumbered. Just as he thought he would be pounced upon at any moment, he heard a loud voice coming from inside the house. He said he would never forget that moment. The voice was Joey's, saying, "I'm coming!" Suddenly he ran out of the house, scooped up Larry over his shoulder, and continued running to bring him to safety. I had never heard that story before. My husband and I both smiled while we choked back our tears.

Larry currently participates in another sport within the college he attends, and he said he has a forethought of Joey each time there is a competition! He said he will never forget him and will be forever grateful for having such a good friend.

It had been over four years since Joey's crossing, at this point in time and still he offers help to many from heaven. It continues to be proven time and time again of Joey's continued loyalty to his family and friends especially in this next example. My elderly Uncle Luke was sent to a convalescent home recently. I had visited him there, and he seemed to be doing as well as expected. Prior to my uncle becoming dependent upon others to care for him, he led a very exciting life. Many years ago, he had been in the entertainment world as an opera singer. He had even performed with a 'noted' entertainer. He was also a gifted athlete in his younger years, very much like Joey.

He participated on the track team and was well-known for throwing the shot put.

As a young man in college my uncle was also a great football player. He, too, received an All State award. His position though was very different, he was a kicker. His philosophy was a kicker never gets hurt! With the knowledge he had and my son playing football also, naturally he wanted to offer whatever he could to help. His hope was to teach Joey his kicking secrets. However, he was living in New York City most of his life and we never found the time prior to Joey's passing. That close bond was never really established as we had wished.

During Uncle Luke's occasional trips to Connecticut, he was able to become more informed of Joey's ability with football. He had always remained very close to his last living sibling, his sister and my Great Aunt Rose. This was either by phone calls to her or a visit when he was in town. So it was here where we would typically have an opportunity to see him. If there happen to be an article at the time, in the newspaper about Joey, I would be sure to point it out to him. Another time when he was in town I invited him to attend Joey's final senior football game during the Championship playoffs. It's a shame that was the only game his senior high school team had lost!

Now though, he had reached eighty-six years of age and was in poor health. We all were concerned for Uncle Luke. The following event showed us how even though Joey had passed away, he was offering help and his uncle meant a great deal to him!

My uncle's health continued to deteriorate as time went by. We sent our love and prayers to him while I solely asked Joey to help him in whatever way he could. It was not too long after that, we learned he was moved to a hospital. We really became worried. My mother and I went to pay him a visit. We were led to a front desk. We asked for his room, and we were sent into another building. Once there, we needed to locate his room number. I asked a nurse, and she picked up a list. She turned to us and said, "Oh, he's in 34!" Just like that, not he's in room 34, or the entire room number, which was actually 1034! Well, you could probably imagine she must have thought I lost my mind because I certainly got the message, and I could not contain my laughter of happiness. My mother returned with a quick comment, "Where else would he be?"

We continued walking down the hallway laughing our heads off. We were very pleased to know Joey was nearby and offering our uncle the love and help he desperately needed at this time.

I have learned through all the reassuring signs of love that he continually supports us. He is aware of our needs and is never bothered by offering us help. It also proves that even though they were not that close in life, it doesn't really matter. Just as Joey loved many in life, he continues to love...from the other side!

CHAPTER 12

THE MISSION

In the face of hopelessness, strength is found
One's footing is regained as an unrelenting push
Finding a purpose and connection, begin to unfold
Satisfaction is found while helping others
To your surprise, you soon discover you are not alone
Miracles happen when we share the burden
And extend ourselves to others.

I began my further spiritual inward quest. Continually I searched to find some direction to help me utilize all my God-given gifts. Now the meditation I had begun as a child needed to begin once again. I began to attend workshops such as Reiki and a few others for my spiritual knowledge and hopeful progression. I purchased CDs and followed guided meditations, so I could once again learn how to relax and hopefully connect directly in some way, to Joey. After some time, I didn't know if I was getting anywhere. Joey had assured Gianna that in time all would come together including a much-anticipated dream of him. A connection of my own is what I truly longed for.

One night I was woken up by my oldest daughter, Isabelle. It was about 5:00 am. It was almost time for me to be getting up for work. She said as she walked past my bedroom she was startled by a large yellowish glowing globe hovering over me as I slept. This new information brought me to a conclusion that I was must be making some kind of progress. I researched this to understand what it was. I learned this is usually a sign of a very much evolved spirit. I thought and hoped it was my Joey. He must have been helping me even more than I thought possible. So I vowed to continue to learn, all that I possibly could.

I went to other seminars with well-known mediums, not because I doubted Marti, but because I needed to squash all those maybes in the world. There is a lot of uncertainty and conflicting information out there. I needed to be able to stand up with my pain and without a doubt, know what is true. I was on a fact-finding mission. This final piece after all of the proof I had would completely put my mind to rest. It would become my salvation even when I was having one of those especially very bad days. My intention was to be completely positive my son was fine and happy in heaven.

I soon had noticed that there was a common thread among all the readings I had attended. Many of the same facts were continually being repeated. Much of the details referring to Joey's passing and other past family members names were exactly the same. They confirmed how he was a helper to those here and on the other side, especially children. Messages were also delivered concerning things that were yet to come. Joey's personality always came through correctly.

How can people without any prior knowledge acquire such accuracy? I came to a conclusion with all of the information that I had received, this clearly is not a conspiracy. I also believe we remain a part of our families and maintain our true personalities after our life on earth, is over. The bond of love is never-ending. With all of the great messages of hope that were delivered, I made a vow to do all that I could. I would continue the bond with my son and help others. Joey has told Gianna that heaven sees all and offers us help in many ways. I truly believe we are all meant to help each other while we are here. Through that, we are giving and receiving love.

I felt so blessed on my continued path of healing, so I knew I needed to extend my newly established hope to others in pain. I joined a support group for grieving parents that have experienced the loss of a child. The group always maintained an open ear among the many others who share their pain and circumstance as well. I noticed the great help such an organization offers.

As I continued to feel stronger, I felt compelled to help others even more. Through friends, I discovered a group of very special individuals within my town who offered support on another level. I was not aware of this support group prior to Joey's passing. I was so taken back as I sat in on my first meeting. The participants explained the upcoming agenda along with all of the help they offered children. As I listened, I heard each one of them give an update to their duties. They were called appropriately the Angels Foundation. The word *angels* stands for Achieving Necessary Goals Emphasizing Loving Support! They help children who are faced with catastrophic or life-altering conditions within our town. Wow! Do they make a difference while touching lives. They offer babysitting, paying hospital bills, reimbursing parents for parking fees during hospital stays for their children, and even helping with fuel costs for the family's car if a child needs care at a distant hospital. How do they do it? Through their dedication with lots of fundraisers and donations to raise money for their cause. I quickly knew I wanted to join their team.

I soon had an idea for raising funds. How about a type of seminar where people received an afternoon filled with hope and joy? I of course was thinking of a Marti gathering. She could deliver readings as John Edward does in his show and donate the funds to the foundation. People would receive messages while helping children at the same time. Marti jumped at the chance to join us in our cause.

A month or two after I joined the Angel's Foundation, Auntie Toni was diagnosed with a form of cancer. Thank God she has always been vigilant with her continuous doctor visits throughout her life! It was during a routine doctor's appointment that the discovery was made. To say the least, we were all devastated once we received the news. I knew we needed to be strong, so I did as I always do: pray! All of the other family members especially her children were also praying for her. I had just begun reading a book about angels by the well-known author, Doreen Virtue. The title of the book is; 'Angels 101.' Within the pages it describes how angels hear us and that we need to ask for their help if we wish for it. So I began asking in a big way! I prayed to the angels and especially to Archangel Raphael. This angel helps the sick and assists the healers of the world.

The day she was to meet with the surgeon who would be doing the operation needed, brought about a very big sign! She was at her daughter's house. She and her daughter and granddaughter were sitting out on the front steps, when they noticed something in the sky. The clouds appeared to be in a strange formation. After they carefully studied them, they were sure it looked very much like an angel. Quickly they snapped a picture, and voila! We had our confirmation of the heavenly help she was receiving. It calmed our fears and we continued our prayers for Aunti Toni.

I was continually processing all of the ideas that were rushing through my head for our fundraiser. I knew first we needed a flier, with Marti's name on it, to get the word out. We also needed to display photos at our fundraiser that would really inspire people. I had the picture in my head of the angel I had seen many times throughout my life. It is of a magnificent angel with very large wings hovering over two children, a boy and a girl, obviously guiding and protecting them. It has similarities to the purpose of our organization. They are crossing a broken bridge, and it appears to be nighttime. There are also fierce lightning bolts running through the sky in the background.

I thought this picture would help to send our message and support our theme. Also, I thought while helping children who face catastrophic health conditions, you need some stability within the turbulent world that surrounds them. I remembered seeing this picture in the past, mostly showing up on posters or in books. No matter how much I searched, I couldn't find this illustration anywhere! I even searched on the computer and still had trouble.

One day as I passed by my bureau in my bedroom, something caught my attention. It was the Sacred Heart of Jesus calendar.

I momentarily thought there would be only religious pictures throughout the pages. Curiously, I opened it and looked through each month. I reached Joey's birth month, July, and there it was!

Then as I studied this photo and put it next to the sky angel picture Auntie Toni's granddaughter took, I was amazed! They had similarities! Wow, now I really had a concrete validation to our passion, being divinely guided. So I was sure to erect it upon a poster board and planned on displaying it during our fundraiser. The electricity of the anticipation filled the room. A few of us gave speeches to inform the audience of what Marti does and how she has helped many, including some of us!

Once I said my few words, I explained about the angel photo that Auntie Toni's grandaughter took and displayed it with the newest angel photo with the children, so all would see the similarities. There was a hush followed by oohs and aahs! Soon, smiles were beaming among many of the people within the audience. It was a great success! We vowed to hold one seminar each year and reach as many needy children as possible. My husband also took on an idea of his own toward helping others while still keeping Joey's name alive. He began the Joe Stone Foundation. His intention was to offer help to high school students.

He held an annual golf tournament, and each and every year, it was sold out. This also was another way of extending the help Joey offered to so many. Only now his dad was honored with the job.

CHAPTER 13

ETERNALLY MINE

A heavenly gift that is eternal
The bonds that must weather a great storm
Though our journey may seem long
Feeling abandoned is ever so overwhelming
In actuality, it is only an illusion of time
They're no further than a thought away
Love remains forever yours.

Still today, I speak to my son each and every day. When times become so overwhelming, I turn to him for help. The spring of 2005, I was preparing for a trip to Disney World with my daughters. This was one of Joey's favorite family vacation destinations. It took a few years to feel up to it enough, to visit again. I did keep in mind, however, that he wouldn't really be far from us.

A few days before we were to leave, I did some last minute shopping. With all of the hectic errands to complete for a vacation, I stopped at a few stores. After an hour or two, I was on my way home when something dawned on me. All of a sudden, I thought I didn't have my credit card. I quickly pulled the vehicle over and checked my purse. I was right; it was missing. Well, I only own one major credit card because I don't like plastic. However, I knew we would definitely need it for our stay in Florida.

So I drove back frantically, thinking about where it might be or who could have found it. I of course feared the worst, so I quickly said a prayer. Then I turned to my son for some heavenly help. I pleaded for him to help me to locate it. So I stopped and went into into one of the stores I had previously been in. I searched, but it was nowhere in sight. I was about to ask an employee and hesitated. All of a sudden, it popped into my mind where it was and where I had lost it. So I rushed back to the large department store parking lot where I had been shopping. I stopped my car and walked over to a spot where I thought I had parked earlier. I looked and looked, still no credit card. I started to walk to my car when something hit me. I stopped in my tracks and looked down at my feet. I certainly never thought it might be found right outside the front door of the store. But there it was, lying right before me! Face up, in plain site within this huge parking lot. Many people surely must have walked by it. I know Joey helped me again, when I called to him and needed him most.

I have found when I really feel like I'm being drawn into a state of overwhelming grief, he reaches me in a way that will touch me so personally. There simply is no denying the message of love I receive from him. Recently, my husband and I have become friends with another couple who lives in a nearby town. Unfortunately, they also have lost a son, Matthew, who had passed away a couple of years after Joey did. We offered them all of the information we have gained to aid them in their journey of grief. They decided they really wanted to contact their son and wished to speak to Marti. So I gave them the phone number, and they made a telephone reading appointment. They wanted to tape the reading, with Marti's permission, and I owned a machine for them to do so.

A few days before the scheduled appointment, the father came to our house to pick up the machine. He had not ever seen any pictures of Joey or any of his football or other sport trophies. My husband showed him everything with great pride. Joe learned that his friend's son, Matthew, had also played a sport; it was hockey. He was a great asset to his team with his talent. We later learned Matthew and Joey did know of each other. Joey had attended many of the high school hockey games and cheered very loudly with his friends. Matthew's team played there as well, and that's how they met.

I had been having a couple of down days and was missing my son a great deal. The anniversary of his death was close. When this dad left, I thought of my son and sent him a private request. I pleaded for Joey to please send me a message, if possible. I knew this family would be helped greatly by the healing messages they would receive, and I was very excited for them. I hoped, though, for just maybe a word or two from my son without taking anything away from this family.

The day of the appointment, I phoned the mom after her reading. She was so elated with her messages. So many facts came through for her and her husband, which removed any doubt of life after death. Then halfway into the reading, she said Marti told her she saw the number 34. I hadn't seen Marti in quite a long time, and this family was from another town. Since her son played a different sport and obviously wore another number, there was no connection to Joey. At first the mom said that the number 34 meant nothing to her. Then the dad, remembering the visit with us a few days earlier at our home, spoke up. "I know who that is, that's my friend's son."

Now Marti, channeling and recalling the spirit of Joey, then recognized who it was. She blurted, "No. I know who this is, and he is telling me he has a message for his mother: tell her I love her."

I was overjoyed as the mom spoke of her healing messages and then also delivered the message to me that I so desperately needed that day. I have confirmation once again. I knew this was truly my son, and he definitely hears me.

Since I have other children attending the high school I needed to drive there often. It was very hard not to notice the football press box where Joey's name is still in plain sight. One day, as I passed it, I recalled the long happy football pasta dinners we had attended there, so many years ago. I recalled how much I missed those days. Then I went on throughout my day, not thinking too much more about it. A day or so later, I was really missing my son. I sent a thought to him of how he hasn't sent a dream to anyone in a while and how much I miss him. Two days later, a friend of Joey's whom he had played football with, called me.

He said, "Mrs. Stone, I had another dream of Joey."

I said, "Okay, what did he say?"

"Not too much," he said.

Then he went on to describe a wonderful dream with a special message for me. He said he, my husband, and I were back in the high school yard, and were attending a football pasta dinner night. Immediately, I said, "I was just thinking of that!" Then he said he was standing next to my husband and I, along with a few others before the dinner outside of the building. All of a sudden, he noticed Joey walking up to him. Joey then leaned over to this friend's ear and whispered, "Give my mom a hug." At first he looked at him a little confused, and Joey made a gesture toward me as he whispered it once more to him. So then he said he hugged me. He turned to Joey for reassurance of fulfilling his request. Joey looked at him with a smile, reached out his hand, and pointed to me, then walked away.

Wow, here is another perfect example of him hearing me very clearly and cleverly designing another unique dream. There is just no denying his constant message of love. There is nothing in the world that can come close to the healing that it delivers; it is an ever deepening support that I feel from him. With this, I continue to realize that my son has never let me down, and he had never left me to pick up the pieces of life again, alone. So I will never let him down and simply embrace his loving support.

The dreams and messages are constantly creating a foundation of greater strength towards survival. I have also been blessed in many other ways that have become my own visual reinforcement.

Joey was honored with an everlasting memorial. A new street was being added to the end of ours. We were approached not very long after his passing and asked if we would like for the street to be named after Joey. How honored we felt and we will be so forever grateful. What recognition for our son! Each time as I drive by, I quickly focus my site upon the sign. I still can't believe my eyes! This street reaches a high-enough peak so that it overlooks the high school. You can even see the football field. The chosen name for the street was perfect: Joe Stone Way. The best part of this was, it is also located right up the street from the home he had grown up in. Hopefully his inspiration for so many, will continue for many years to come.

My journey has taken me down a road enabling me to meet many others in similar circumstances. It has given me the opportunity to create bonds I may not have made if the tragic event had not occurred. Don't misunderstand me; I certainly would have leapt at any means to not have endured the pain of my son's crossing. But as time goes on, I continue to often locate the hidden gifts that are becoming exposed as I continue to heal. These gifts must be meant for helping others. Unknowingly, these bonds of new friendships have led to unexpecting love and support from others, which helps to spread awareness. Keeping that in mind, makes my road a little easier.

CHAPTER 14

BUT DOES HE MISS ME?

Soon after Joey's passing, this question weighs heavy on my mind. Over and over I repeat to myself, "How can he not miss me?" The wonderful talks we had, the understanding between us. The bond of love that once was does still exist and remains so very precious to me. Such as the love for his dad and sisters, I cannot imagine him not missing that.

When I presented these questions to Gianna as she spoke to Joey, he always said, "Yes, I miss you all, Mom." I believe we miss the conscious fluent and verbal line of communication that was so comforting and is no longer the same. Now it has changed, and we must recognize the signs of communication in a new and unfamiliar way. I'm convinced that, as we return to heaven, our deepest desires will be met, and we will realize they were with us and they heard us always. It is the *love* that they never miss, because we give and receive it continuously.

CHAPTER 15

A MOTHER'S LOVE

Strength, Faith, Hope
The undying love for our children never diminishes, it
intensifies
If your child is physically no longer present
Stop and close your eyes; you can feel them enveloping you
Celebrate their love and speak of them often
Not in whispers, acknowledge them out loud
Believe they can hear your every word
God has entrusted them to you
Remember, not only are they a gift
So are you!
Their spirit lingers close by, *forever*
None can compare to a mother's unconditional love!
They are eternally ours.

CHAPTER 16

A LESSON LEARNED

It is often said we plan our entry into the world prior to our birth. I often wonder, why do we create our earthly hardships? What would compel me to leave heaven and struggle here in this school of life, while enduring such monumental pain? *What was I thinking?* I believe that while we all come here for many different lessons, there is only one that we all are here to learn: love. To understand what it truly means. Learning this through loss, seems to be the hardest and most unforgettable lesson of all. Because of this, I have become even more aware of how precious the gift of love is. Not that I wasn't aware before, but the impact delivered through this all-encompassing and debilitating pain has burned this understanding deep within my soul forever. There remains no question; love exceeds all else.

I now firmly believe leaving our heavenly home has a great purpose and plan always to better ourselves as well as others within our lives. We then transform ourselves into hopeful heroes accepting these especially difficult achievements. Talk about raising the bar! Many are among us experiencing great loss. Those who are living it and surviving are the ones who understand. Through my loss being ever so deep, I can truly say, "I get it. Lesson learned."

Thank you, my Joey

CHAPTER 17

FOUND HOPE BECOMES MY TRUTH

I believe everyone needs to find their own niche within them, which transforms into a unique survival tool. It's really what works for them that matters. All I can provide is what works for me.

One of the hardest things for me to do since Joey's passing was, visiting the grave site. No matter how many times I forced myself there, it seemed to increase my pain. It wasn't a denial thing either, because nothing could make me forget the brutal truth. It wasn't until I walked this road, that I realized these visits are felt by us as an obligation to our loved ones. However, I have come to the realization that they, on the other side, are with us anyways, and they truly don't want to see us becoming more acutely affected by the thoughts of a cold gravesite haunting us. I decided through all I had learned that I knew it was more important to embrace the fact that he was still with me, than to constantly visit a gravesite, which holds an empty vessel that no longer contains my precious son. Birthdays and holidays, are the few times I do visit though.

On Christmas, to honor and respect our son, my husband and I place a beautiful cemetery blanket upon his grave. At home, I hang a stocking for him so we will always remember him and acknowledge him within our family. Our gift then becomes a letter of love I write along with any other family members that feel comfortable enough with it. We know somehow he will get it.

Another belief I have come to embrace is, as it has been said by many others, "No one ever dies alone." There are always loved ones waiting to receive us once we make our transition. A common belief is when we are born; our spiritual family sees us depart while our earthly family is very elated to receive us. The opposite is true when we die; our spiritual family is happy to receive us, and it is then our earthy family's turn to grieve. Another coping mechanism I developed, was to create an unbreakable boundary to protect my heart from outside debilitating influences.

I do not and probably will not ever be comfortable with hearing another's attempt to help me with the so overused phrase "Move on." Come on now, when we love and physically lose someone (especially a child) while on earth, *there really is no moving on!*

My philosophy has become this: holding on to a faith that this venture on earth is really a two-fold deal. We each have a role. The person who is now on the other side has completed his or her role. Yours is not finished, but that doesn't mean you are still not connected to them as you continue your work here. It's like holding up your part of the agreement while learning and teaching, along with others within your life. You must continue your work while retaining your strength, through what still is a love connection. I cannot continue in life without honoring that forever. I trust someday when we meet again, the pieces of life will all be joined together, and we will understand our portion of the puzzle.

Yet still sometimes I am confronted with inquisitive people who ask me very blunt, cold, and hurtful questions. I stop, look them in the eye, and search for strength to answer them. It is hard not to jump down their throat, but clearly they do not realize how their words affect me. I calmly reply, after collecting myself for a brief moment in a self-assured voice, "My son is always with me. Through his love I continue, and I know he will be waiting for me when it's my time." That always works and swiftly ends the conversation. It's obvious; they clearly are at a loss for words.

My vow is held securely toward life as I completely embrace it always. Although my son's physical departure ended through a tragedy, he is *not* the tragedy. *He is the gift!* The gift Joey continues to offer me bears fruit throughout my life. It offers me daily strength, to face life again.

I can honestly say, I no longer cringe within as I find myself becoming happy again. I discovered my first notion of remaining in a "forever grief" mode is kind of a believed self-punishment, I can choose to be forever indebted to. Deep within me, I know my son would not want me to harbor that unfounded guilt for my survival. I am not trivializing my tremendous loss as a mere and brief heartache. My loss is as deep as any mothers could be. I love my son more than anyone can imagine. Instead as I open my heart to him completely, it aides me further in discovering more and more of my own strength. This is a road I know my son would want and expect me to take. I truly feel it honors his love. A gift I want to return to him. I shall forever try to match the vast amount he has given me!

I have come to discover that being strong is not the only thing for our surviving children's happiness. To continually reassure them of your unbroken and unconditional eternal love for them also, is what they need to feel more than ever! Reinforce the love they receive equally. Their need can somehow become less visible to you as you are trying to heal yourself toward your now forever-changed lives. Their value should be showered upon them and overflowing with love. I feel this is empowering them to love themselves, along with the many within their own lives. And as I turn to Joey, I attempt to fully absorb and continue this also within his message of love and hope.

CHAPTER 18

THE WINDING ROAD FINALLY BECOMES A WIDE AND SMOOTH PATH

As time evolves, I eventually realize I had the key all along as my quest begins to lead me in another direction. More pieces of the puzzle continually are falling into place.

Many times I have heard the words "To help with the healing of others, we first must allow healing of our own grief." I never really understood that statement. Now as some time has passed, I feel like the fog is lifting, and I have a better understanding of what those words actually meant. I recall in the past, one of the ways I dealt with the weight of my pain. I found myself sometimes storing it away on a shelf, without even realizing it. It was kind of like, just slicing it off of me as if it didn't exist. As I joined grief support groups, I noticed this in others as well. However when I do receive heavenly messages, which I feel are extremely helpful, that is not where it all ends. Yes, they do propel you into a realm of hope, while attempting to speed up the healing. Although unfortunately, there is no quick fix because this is truly a process.

Then as I focused on myself, I'd remember some of the deep stages of emotion I experienced. Even as the little amount of details revealed to me of that tragic day terrorized my thoughts, I still somehow found a way to cope. I found a way to accept what details

I could and then to throw up an impenetrable wall of protection against all the rest. A wall to protect me from the pain, a pain I could not possibly bear at the time. Little did I know then that to some degree, this included hindering my anticipated dream visitation. Maybe that's why I always heard, "You are not ready." "Mom, you need to open your heart and let me in," delivered by Gianna from Joey.

So I think I know what those words meant. I had the key to my eventual dream all along. But I was actually, too afraid of not being able to handle it. This again proves that everyone deals with grief in different stages. Maybe it was all supposed to happen this way, so I would push myself to learn as much as possible on my earthly mission. I've learned it is part of the process, and since now I have an answer, maybe it was time to implement it. I only needed to build my courage.

As I was continually pursuing this new path, I began to fine-tune my target through new and revealing ways, many of which I had not previously thought of. First, I realized I had more help here in the growing friendships I was discovering. A girl named Connie, who didn't live very far from my home and who had also experienced the loss of a child, became my dear friend. I had met her at a bereaved parent support group meeting. We were able to share our feelings of grief and support, and even our beliefs were rapidly developing toward the same thing; believing in the afterlife. It didn't take too long after meeting her that I shared my Gianna story. I guess that's where we began to make our connection discovery. She too told me she had seen Marti, and she was a great help to her also. I soon was confiding in Connie and knew she was truthful, and finally I could count on another outside source. She then was confiding in me of her and also her child's ability: to see spirit. We really did seem to have a lot in common.

Soon she introduced me to a great friend of hers, named Stephanie. She too had lost a child and was just as nice as Connie. We formed a threesome to support each other and decided together, that we would learn as much as we could.

I did already attend many informational spiritual workshops alone like Reiki, but had not found my correct niche yet. My friends and I had heard of this Energy Practitioner that was also within the therapeutic field. I recall when Joey had hurt his shoulder during his high school junior year of football and another teammate's mom informed me of her. She mentioned how her son had an injury and was greatly helped by her intervention. Joey made an appointment, and the treatments he received seemed to have helped him.

I had discovered that this Energy Practitioner, named Colleen, was having a demonstrative energy healing seminar and I decided to attend. I invited my two new friends. Up until that moment, I had never met Colleen. (Joey always drove himself to the appointments, since I was working.) And Colleen certainly had no idea I was going. She did this meditative thing and then approached each and every person and gave them a short reading of their issues in life, along with important information on their health. She seemed to be breathing deeply and doing a lot of sweating. Even though it was warm within the building, she was the one who was clearly feeling it the most.

My friends and I, didn't really know what to make of this. It seemed a little weird, but we kept an open mind. We were kind of used to the weird stuff by then! When she approached me, she instantly knew I was a grieving parent, and I said, "Yes, my son's name is Joey Stone, and you helped him after his shoulder injury." She looked at me, astonished, and said, "Oh yes, I remember." Then she continued to say how he was there helping me and even her. She told me how Joey helps others. She then gave wonderful information to my two friends. We looked at each other and said, "We have to learn this!" We thought now we could turn our loss into something very positive while helping others. This would also help us feel that we were connecting further to our children. This shortly became our new path and passion, as Colleen told us we could sign up and join her upcoming workshops. She would reveal to us, all she knew! The first day was a few months away, and we eagerly waited for it to arrive.

CHAPTER 19

A HUGE CRACK IN THE DOORWAY
OF MY EARTHLY MISSION

As the timing seemed right, the road became more evident.
I knew there was an abundance of promise
Waiting for me as it begins to unfold.

Day one was here, and it would be a full Saturday workshop. Connie was able to join, but Stephanie could not make it due to her job, so instead she would attend at another time. As I looked around the room, I noticed there were only maybe nine or ten people, but I knew two of them! One was another football player's mom. Her son, Alex, was also a captain on the North Branford team, with Joey! The other person was a Sports Medicine Therapist who assisted the North Branford school football players when Joey and Alex were there! Oh my God! This is getting even weirder!

Then after we introduced ourselves, I spoke about my loss and mentioned Joey and how Marti has helped me. I explained how I now felt like, I needed to learn this form of energy healing. Then another mom stood up and said how she had a daughter who was in the same high school with Joey. She further said how Joey did such wonderful things and continued to give him such praise! Wow, I was really moved and felt that I belonged there. Maybe this was the place I had been searching for, and Joey led me here!

After a long day of listening to all the information Colleen gave us, it was time to try energy healing ourselves. I was a little worried, but decided I would give it all I could. I was paired up with another girl. I began the healing technique, Colleen had instructed. At first, I just went through the regimented motions, but then after a short time, my hands were shaking uncontrollably. I felt a sensation that I had never felt before. Colleen noticed and was quickly by my side to help and take over, since I was clearly in over my head at the time. After that day, I knew this was amazing, because that indescribable feeling was so strong. Connie and I even practiced on each other in our homes. It would be some time before we would complete our learning, but we decided to stay dedicated to it.

Colleen explained how this energy healing is becoming more recognized by many hospitals. Wow, I thought, how awesome. She went on to explain how every ailment begins in our expanded energy fields, which we are all surrounded by. As we go through our lives and we don't entirely deal with our emotions and traumas, they affect our energy fields. When we do not face them or clear them, it eventually effects the physical body. The belief is that this is where illness is created. Energy sessions can help people by assisting and removing stagnant energy while charging their fields. We also learned of another benefit of an energy session was that it can help with mental, spiritual and emotional healing. This all will help a person progress toward a healthy self.

With all this new information in mind, we began to practice on our family members. Once I felt a little confident, I offered the healing to anyone who needed it and was willing. I offered it to people with emotional issues and others with serious health issues. After a year or so of practicing, I was informed of a family member who just discovered she was ill. My cousin Julie had just been diagnosed with breast cancer, and she was completely devastated. I wanted to offer whatever I could, so I mentioned the energy sessions to her. She was receptive to it, and I knew she would benefit from it. So soon we saved a date, and I did the session. She expressed how wonderful it made her feel. Julie also shared a story with me that day. She said she had been praying to God and to her cousin Joey, to help her. One day, she had stopped at a store and ran into a young man; then for some reason they began talking. He mentioned he was from North Branford and he seemed to be close to what Joey's age would be. She asked him if he had known, Joey Stone. He said, "Yes, I was two years behind him, and we were friends." He said his name was Mike and told her how Joey had given him a nickname. He said everyone called him by his nickname after that, and it really stuck.

He continued to explain how one day, after he graduated from high school, he had come into contact with a very small kitten. This kitten would not leave him alone, and he felt a pull and strange recognition toward him, which he could not explain at that time. He tried to locate an owner, but the kitten wasn't wearing a collar, and he didn't want to leave him. So he then brought this kitten home. Since he was to leave for college soon, his father questioned him why he had decided to bring home a kitten and would not be there to care for it.

He replied, "Dad, we have to keep this kitten, I just know it." He then named the kitten, Joey. A few months later, he found himself on the football team at college. He received a jersey with the number 34 on it. He told Julie that he had the feeling that Joey was somehow still connected to him. For Julie, she felt she had received a message through all of this and that Joey hears her prayers. She went on to say how she feels he is especially with her during this challenging health condition. Why else would she have run into a complete stranger who spoke of Joey?

CHAPTER 20

THE STORY OF GABRIEL

One day I was left a voice message by an acquaintance to inform me that her son, Gabriel, was unable to attend a local event (I had previous plans to drive him there along with several others). This, at first, sounded like a typical message, until I realized something was very wrong. I then listened closely to the continuing message and soon noticed her voice had an unfamiliar quiver in it. She went on to say his absence was due to a sudden discovery; he was diagnosed with a serious health condition. I was so shocked and upset after the message ended. I called the mother later that day, and she explained to me that Gabriel had been to a doctor recently, and during a routine checkup they realized something was very wrong. A further series of tests concluded the diagnosis. I then offered my friendship and support to her and the family. A week or so went by, and I ran into Gabriel. He was quick to talk about his condition and share his fears with me. All I could do was to encourage him while attempting to find the right words of comfort to express.

I remember speaking to Gabriel concerning some religious items I had at home. I had prayer cards and even some holy water I received during a trip I had been on in Canada, when I visited the Basilica of Sainte-Ann-de-Beaupre' in Quebec City. This is where many miraculous healings occurred throughout the years. Crutches literally were hung on the walls of previous visitors that no longer needed them after their visit. So I offered him my religious items and hoped it would ease some of his fears. He was so grateful. I included him within my own prayers. I also started a special novena prayer to Saint Padre Pio (a well-known healer and saint). Novena prayers are known to have a special strength and are recited in repetition for a number of days. So I began this immediately.

One night, Gabe's mom called me from the hospital. She said Gabriel had been admitted to have a preliminary procedure performed, and as expected, Gabe was petrified. The doctors had explained the risks to him in brutal detail, which further heightened his fear. He was very upset as he was wheeled into the operating room. He was at the point of hysteria when he closed his eyes. But he said something wonderful happened. He saw the face of Jesus Christ, and he was smiling at him. Gabe said once that had happened, he suddenly became very calm. The operation was a success, and later he told the nurses and doctors of his experience. Some of them were very moved by his story.

One night not long after, my daughter Gabrielle, who was a good friend of Gabriel's, and I had stopped at a nearby grocery store for a few items our family needed. It was an unusual time to be doing this type of shopping; however, my day had been very demanding, and it was on my to-do list.

Gabrielle and I finished our shopping and headed out of the store. When we reached the beginning of the parking lot, we both noticed Gabriel's mother, Mary. She was just sitting there in her vehicle, so I approached her to offer some kind and compassionate words of support.

When I drew closer, it was clear to me that she was very upset and was speaking on her cell phone. She noticed me and quickly opened her window. I instantly held her hand and tried to deliver some words of comfort. She began to explain how the recent surgery had revealed other undesirable health complications for Gabriel and this delivered a further frightening prognosis. As she spoke, it was clear how distraught she was. I was sure to keep a completely open ear for her. I still had her hand in my grasp, and I suddenly felt my legs begin to tremble. This was a familiar sensation I quickly recognized as energy healing. So I focused on it; then soon I felt a sensation run up my body and to her hand, that I continued to hold. Mary went on to explain how the doctors were deciding upon a risky procedure. She also said, how she was so frightened when the doctor explained all that would be involved. We spoke for a short time after that, and then Gabrielle and I hugged her before we left.

Further conversations were spoken over the phone, and it was then that I felt secure enough to explain the energy healing I had been learning. She said she was open to it and would allow me to offer this to Gabriel. Once agreed upon, we came up with a date and time that would work for us.

I did the first energy session with him and then with his mother. It was a short session so they could become familiar with it. I touched him lightly, allowing the healing to flow to him. When I removed my hands, Gabriel turned to his mother and said, "Wow, Mom, I felt that throughout my body. I felt tingling and heat, even my headache subsided." Then they both agreed how the feeling was very soothing as this wave of relaxation and peacefulness consumed them.

I called my friend Marti, and she also suggested we pray to the healer Saint Padre Pio. He had pierced palms that bled and replicated Jesus Christ's wounds, during Padre Pio's time on earth. He wore gloves that are now shared among many churches to touch, well after his passing. It has now become well known of the many miraculous healings occurring after a person touches one of these gloves.

I recalled a time years ago when a friend had invited me to join her at such a gathering. Once there, I met a kind couple, named Paul and Marie, who were in care of Padre Pio's glove and had brought it to many local churches. They prayed and touched many people who had attended, in hope of finding healing. People stood in a long line waiting to be touched by the glove, while being prayed over by them and others. Some people would just melt to the floor as a sense of blissful love and peace came over them. While others still waiting in line, whispered stories of miracles that occurred with people who had visited previously. But everyone left with a sense of great peace. I called my friend for the couple's phone number and then called them. I explained Gabriel's condition to Paul. He said they would be happy to meet me at Gabriel's house and pray for him, along with bringing the glove.

The night we agreed on arrived quickly, and I was very excited. The couple came, and I felt instant electricity when they entered Gabe's home. The evening was amazing as I just felt the abundance of love that surrounded us all. As the glove was placed on Gabriel, a prayer was said and was soon followed by a short song. The entire night really gave a boost to everyone's hope for Gabe's healing. After finishing with the family, Paul and Marie placed the glove over my heart and then pressed it to my hands. I immediately felt a sense of peace. The family was so grateful, and everyone hugged each other before Paul and Marie left. I went home that night just in awe. Fast approaching was the date Gabriel was to have yet another operation. He and his mother requested another energy session. This time, I asked the both of them if I could invite my friend Connie.

Since Connie was able to sense and communicate with spirit, I knew she would be able to offer any reassurance she received. Gabe and his mom agreed, so we set a date for the upcoming weekend.

The day arrived for the next energy session. Connie and I arrived at Gabe's, while feeling very honored to offer what we had learned. We were aware the following day would be the operation, and Gabe was understandably very nervous due to the seriousness of the risks involved.

Connie began with the energy session at Gabriel's head and explained all that she saw. I began my session at his feet. Immediately, Connie said she sees Joey. She said he showed up with his football uniform on and brought along a friend. (I did not recognize her description of this person.) I whispered quietly to Joey, "I am glad you are here. Please help us with Gabriel." (I love knowing he works with me while helping people.) Then Connie said she sees an Aunt

Mia who has come to help Gabriel also. (This name was unfamiliar to Gabe's mother.) Connie went on to deliver all she was receiving.

"Mia is very protective of Gabe and watching over him", Connie explained. "She was very strong-willed in life and the same holds true in spirit." (Mary researched at a later date and discovered she was on Gabe's father's side of the family. She had crossed over before Gabe was born.) Everything else that was said about her personality was true. Then Connie heard a name—Eric. She didn't see him but only heard the name. She said, "you know he could be helping Gabe also." We finished our session, and Connie gave them one more message that she heard. She announced, "They are saying he will be fine tomorrow and not to worry."

The next day, Gabriel's grandmother (on his dad's side) came to the hospital. Gabe's mother asked for more confirmation about this Aunt Mia. This Grandma agreed with all Connie had said about her. Gabe's mom was very moved by all of this comforting information. Then, the next thing they knew, a young man approached them and spoke directly to Gabe. He went on to introduce himself, "Hi, my name is Eric. I will be your nurse, and I am going to take very good care of you!"

Well, you can imagine that they all stood in shock, but Gabe's mom found comfort in this, since now she really believed he would survive the operation. She knew he was in good heaven-sent hands.

Hours had passed, and Gabe's mom and family waited patiently. Soon he was strolled out into the recovery room, and he was talking! The doctors were pleased with his quick awareness. I realized there were two sides to all the messages the family had received. It was not only for Gabe's benefit but also for his mom to hold herself together through this. I felt so honored to be a witness to it all. In a month, Gabe returned to his school! The doctors told him he was a miracle!

CHAPTER 21

I FOLLOW ANOTHER BEND IN THE ROAD WHILE FEEDING THE HUNGER THAT CONTINUALLY DRIVES ME

My friend Connie e-mailed me one day with information on an upcoming hypnotherapy workshop. She thought we should give it a try. So I thought about it. I did always have an interest in this and found it fascinating. I also thought it may help us connect to our children somehow. Connie, Stephanie, and I signed up. It would start in a few weeks.

The day of our hypnotherapy workshop had arrived and we were filled with the euphoria of a new venture on our paths toward more knowledge. How exciting it was! The three of us traveled together and spoke of it with such anticipation throughout the entire ride. Before we exited the car, we reaffirmed our pact to stay connected so we each would absorb every detail.

We eagerly entered the small building and quickly located seats within a prepared room. Our instructor entered and introduced himself, and each one of us did also, on his cue. The group was small, which I think helped us all to feel comfortable.

Soon all the steps were carefully explained and we began to practice on each other. I felt a little weird and was somewhat unsure of how it all really worked, but I remained committed to absorb as much as possible with an open mind. I realized it all seemed to hinge on the ability to relax, which I definitely needed to achieve. This I hoped would strengthen my communication with Joey and ultimately lead to my long-awaited dream. After a session, I noticed I found it hard to let go and just allow my mind to rest. However, my friends seemed to have a little easier time with the whole process, especially Stephanie.

At one point, a few weeks later during the third workshop, the instructor did a demonstration on her! We were all fascinated as soon as the instructor began to induce a hypnotic state of awareness on Stephanie. Immediately it appeared as if she had nodded off right before our eyes, while still standing up! We looked at each other in amazement; we could hardly believe it! It was truly shocking, but this proved to us that this really is actually achievable. As the classes continued the experimenting came with more and more surprises. Each time I practiced, I felt the ability to relax and letting go became a little easier.

A workshop partner named Annie, who was also a Reiki master, asked to share a session of hypnotherapy with me. I agreed, and before it, I reminded myself to allow all I could to receive the most from it. She had soft music playing, which further seemed to help me to let my guard down. Then she began, and I saw myself on a beach, but I was a man! Then I felt like I was Joey, climbing rocks to the top of a cliff! (I knew this is what he had done on that tragic day, prior to swimming.) Well, I lost it, and I began to become very emotional and sobbed through the rest of the session. The waves of grief washed over me; it seemed to open something I had locked away. Annie was very understanding and helpful, and she spoke caringly to me until I calmed down. I believe it helped to further point me in the right direction. I later learned that all the others in the workshop were having great breakthroughs during their sessions also.

As we approached the end of all our workshops, the instructor allowed us to construct a session while including a special addition he had taught us. So this time, Stefanie and I teamed up and would attempt this addition, which was called a script (the main idea) within the hypnotherapy session. We were allowed to pick our own, instead of the generic one he had us using previously. I then searched a book the instructor had and located a script that drew my attention. It described walking through a beautiful forest. I liked the feeling I received by just reading it quickly. I would allow Stephanie to try this session on me first.

When she began, it initially seemed similar to some of the other scripts we had experimented with, until she reached the end. I was a little disappointed since I didn't really see anything; however, I did have a subtle sensation familiar to being with Joey. That then really raised my curiosity, and I didn't hesitate to try it on Stephanie.

Stephanie seemed to easily relax as I started the session. As I approached the very end, she gasped and then let out a sob! I was a little confused at the moment until she announced to me, "I see my daughter, and she is happy and beautiful!" It was amazing! It felt so wonderful to be a part of helping her with this connection. When all of the others were finished, we told the instructor about it with excitement. (We learned he had lost a child also.) It seemed to have even reached him with some sense of relief. It was definitely an unforgettable afternoon.

CHAPTER 22

THE PIECES OF HOPE COMING TOGETHER

My new found path as a healer was now born upon joey's wings.I came to an epiphany and enlightenment. I came through the storm of my greatest pain and realized that Joey's life was not lost but found alive and well! And through all of the many signs, messages and people he speaks through, he also taught me "why" he had to leave this earth while validating his continued existence. As an old soul my Joey came into this world to touch as many lives as possible in loving and life altering ways. He had a soul purpose… a job to do and he did it ,oh so well. He was a champion for the underdog but also a true champion to everyone he met, knew and loved. He was selfless and courageous and gave of himself unconditionally. He loved and was so loved by so many and his legacy lives on. We are strong and proud to be a united family and I'm especially humbled to say my son passed his torch onto me. To do good in this world and to rise above my pain and offer myself to helping others who also suffer. I never thought in a million years I would be thinking, believing and doing the things I am doing today, but I'm honored to say Joey opened up that Universal… Heavenly door for me to walk through, following in his footsteps.

EPILOGUE

God's Will
One day, when the time is right
God will call me home
Joey will be there waiting within the light
He will take me by the hand, ever so gently
I will fall deeply into his welcoming and loving arms
While basking within an emanating immense and blissful
joy
Only then will I truly know
Heaven!
He lived life to change lives
And crossed over to do the same
Until then, my endless faith
Tells me, he is always
Eternally mine.

AFTERWORD

MY SKY ANGEL

I was completing the final touches on my book, and I was in the process of copying the angel photo that was taken when my aunt was sick. As I temporarily took a short break, I began to fill my mind with all that I was learning about angels. I looked forward to the day when I would be joining a Doreen Virtue event.

A few days earlier, I attended a workshop given by a woman who had recently received certification through Doreen Virtue. She mentioned how to ask for signs from angels as she had done and was explained in the book *Angels 101*. She had mentioned all of her encounters with signs, and I was very intrigued. So of course, I did it! I would remember this day because I was not praying as I had with Auntie Toni's illness. This was just simply asking for a sign. You would think the other photo was convincing enough for me.

I was determined to get back to my book, but I remembered something I needed upstairs. As I stopped upon the top landing and peered out the front door, for some reason my attention was drawn upward. Well, I was in disbelief and rubbed my eyes as I focused on the clouds. I thought for a minute my eyes were playing games on me or I was just hoping at that point to see another angel. As I continued to look, I knew there was no doubt about it, the cloud formation was definitely too organized to appear as anything else. Then I didn't waste a minute and found my camera quickly. I snapped and snapped as many pictures as I possibly could. I even went outside and followed it, while it moved across the sky and over my house! I snapped and snapped until it faded away.

To my surprise, that wasn't my only sign. On my way home from work the next day, I was behind a car that had a sticker on the side of it. It said, "I believe in angels!"

And another sticker just said, "Angels." I was beginning to really becoming angel crazy. After all, this too was further validation while still dealing with my grief. I thought to myself, this was more proof of the goodness that exists in the afterlife.

Further on my way home, there was still one more sign. While waiting at a red light, I noticed a car coming toward me with a license plate that said, "Angel." Wow, I thought to myself, another sign! It wasn't until a few days later that something further dawned on me. The sky angel was in perfect formation as the angel statue I have in front of my home. This statue is located right near Joey's footstone outside my door. (His friends had given us this gift of love right after his passing.) The only difference is the sky angel was appropriately wearing a large cloud halo! I feel somehow Joey must have been included in this last revelation. Surely, it is a sign of how much we *all* are *loved*!

Believe!

There were many other occurrences,

They all could not possibly be contained within this book.

Many signs and dreams still continue today.

Although our heavenly visits have diminished temporarily,

Joey's love can be counted on always.

My husband, myself, and our other children

remain strongly united in our belief of

all of the heavenly visits and messages.

Marti and I have truly become dear friends,

I am forever thankful,

and I love her more than words can say.

The mention of her name has continued

to become infectious to many.

Once you receive a dose of her healing messages,

you can't wait to tell others.

Now as I read through my completed book,

It still continues to reinforce my own strength

and direction within my life.

I continue to wait for my dream visit,

Maybe now I am strong enough to handle it.

He has promised, and it will happen.

This I know because Joey keeps his promises.

However, I have decided to surrender my wish to God.

As my story continues to unfold,

I now know his love has led me forward,

toward a new direction.

May we all recognize the love within our own lives.

I hope it has brought peace and most of all hope

to all as it has for us.

Love lives!

"A UNITING COURAGE LIES WITHIN THE
HEART OF A HERO"

JOSEPH NICHOLAS STONE

http://mariannestone.tateauthor.com